D1557817

TO DIE WELL

STEPHEN E. DORAN, M.D.

To Die Well

*A Catholic Neurosurgeon's
Guide to the End of Life*

IGNATIUS PRESS   SAN FRANCISCO

To my beloved wife, the rose of Sharon,
a lily of the valleys, who illumines
the art of living well by serving the Word.

"I am my beloved's and my beloved is mine."

—Song of Songs 6:3

Contents

Preface

I have been a neurosurgeon for over twenty-five years, and despite the inevitability of death, most of my patients and their families have largely ignored its inescapable reality.

I think we all want a "good" death, but we are not really sure what that means or how to prepare for it. Some of my patients die suddenly and unexpectedly. Some have months of advance notice. Many are somewhere between. Regardless, they—along with the rest of us—want to do this last thing right. We want to die well. We want our loved ones to die well. Yet, there is not a formula or a one-size-fits-all plan for a good death. As there is an art of medicine, there is an art to dying well.

As a deacon, a physician, and an ethicist I accompany patients and their families as they navigate the complex spiritual, medical, and moral challenges that come with the process of dying. My purpose in writing this book is to draw from my experiences and to present the Catholic perspective on the art of dying well, while answering some of the common questions that arise. My hope is that this book will not only answer questions, but also give readers pause, moving them to contemplate, pray about, and prepare for the end of their earthly lives.

Introduction

Like most kids, I never really thought much about death. Why should I? Being a kid meant being alive—playing kick-the-can, watching *Gilligan's Island*, mooching a cookie, doing homework, grumbling through chores. On rare occasions, death intruded for a moment, but never really made an impact. Death was an excuse to get pulled out of class, serve at a funeral Mass, eat some ham, and pocket a few dollars given in thanks. Death was obscure, distant. Death was an uncle I never really knew. Even when one of my grandparents passed away, it all seemed abstract, sterile, as if I were watching a boring documentary. And so it went through high school and college.

You would think that medical school would have made death more real. After all, the first week of class begins with an introduction to your cadaver for the year. If a cadaver couldn't make death real, what else could? Interestingly, dissecting a cadaver had the exact opposite effect. Maybe it was a natural defense mechanism, but I never really saw this body as a person. The body in front of me was a collection of formalin-saturated parts and pieces that my inept hands crudely separated, split open, and eventually discarded. If I had stopped to consider that this body was the remains of a person, maybe I would have stopped altogether under the weight of that revelation.

Neurosurgery residency was a jarring awakening to the reality of death. In medical school, I read about death. In residency, I witnessed death on a weekly, if not daily, basis. I trained at a large university hospital that cared for the sickest of the sick. The neuro ICU was full of patients with malignant brain tumors, ruptured aneurysms, massive head injuries. Often, the task of communicating with family members was delegated to the residents, as the faculty neurosurgeons maintained their distance. Coming face to face with grieving spouses and children was an ongoing punch in the gut. Death was tragic, often unanticipated, and seldom contemplated in advance. While death was undoubtedly more real to me at this point, it remained uncoupled from life. It was a separate event that occurred at the end of life, rather than a brilliant thread woven into a rich tapestry.

Mike Lewandowski changed all that. Mike was my father-in-law, father to five daughters and two sons. An honest, hardworking telephone repairman, Mike lived a life of holiness that crescendoed to a glorious death. Mike was the head of the household in a truly biblical sense. He showered his children with love, he expected them to act with virtue, and he loved his wife, Mary Ann, with the sacrificial love of Ephesians 5:25–26: "Husbands, love your wives, as Christ loved the Church, and gave himself up for her, that he might sanctify her, having cleansed her by the washing of water with the word."

Before Mike's final illness, I don't have a particular memory of him talking about death (although no doubt he did). But Mike lived ready. He anticipated his earthly end and lived accordingly. Some might say that Mike's life was cut short when he died at age seventy, but I would beg to differ. His life came to completion.

When it was discovered that Mike had an aggressive leukemia, he was immediately hospitalized, and chemotherapy was initiated. The poisons meant to cure him caused his skin to slough from his palms and blisters to form inside his mouth, making it incredibly painful to grasp the spoon that brought soup to his mouth, which could barely open to receive nourishment. Yet, in spite of his suffering, Mike never complained. Ever.

When it was clear the treatments were futile, Mike went home to die. And everyone else went home with him. A simple three-bedroom house was instantly transformed into a makeshift hotel housing his children and dozens of his grandchildren. The entrance to his home was a revolving door of visitors wanting to catch one last moment with this holy man, to receive his blessing, and to share a moment of quiet prayer.

As Mike continued to decline, he was confined to his deathbed, which, in all reality, was his life bed. No idle chitchat. Only prayer, song, and Scripture. Death drew ever closer, and on his final day, Mike was surrounded by his wife and children as they prayed the Rosary. Just as the final mystery was completed, Mike breathed his last and died. He was buried on August 15, the feast of the Assumption of Mary. Mike died a good death. Why? What was good about it? It was good because the spiritual realities of death were not pushed aside but embraced, welcomed—not only by Mike, but also by his family.

Modern society has a paradoxical attitude toward death. On the one hand, death is hidden away, not talked about, taboo. On the other hand, death is put on display in violent movies, games, and even popular songs, not to mention the nightly news. Mostly, death is something that happens to someone else in some other place. When it does come to our door, all too often the physical process of death and the

medical attempts to stop it eclipse the spiritual transforma-
tion and transition that is taking place. But it does not have
to be this way. Mike showed me that.

So, before going further, we must draw back and ask
ourselves, What is death? What happens when we die? The
physical realities of death answer only one portion of that
question, and that part of the equation is not all that mysterious. However, death is more than the cessation of bodily
functions. Death is the departure of the soul from the body,
and that is incredibly mysterious and deserves more atten-
tion and preparation. Unfortunately, the spiritual realities of
death are often largely ignored when the focus is on stopping
the decline of the body. Death has become medicalized: illness and death are the enemy, and modern technologies are
the weapons to defeat them. In the battle against death, the
patient is often reduced to an interested bystander whose
humanity or personhood is largely ignored.

When a person is in the hospital, he is a medical problem
to be solved. His attending doctor and other members of
the team "round" on him and their other patients. During
rounds, labs, scans, vital signs, and so on are reviewed; a
plan is developed. Almost as an afterthought, the team en-
ters the patient's room and inquires how things are going;
they briefly examine him, present their plan, allow a few moments for questions, and then move on to the next room.
No time to linger. No time to visit. But the gravely ill person needs more than this. Much more. There are serious
moral and spiritual matters to consider in order to help a
person prepare for death.

The purpose of this book is to address those important yet
often overlooked considerations. The first part focuses on
moral questions that surround death and dying, including

end-of-life medical decisions and topics such as suicide and euthanasia. The second part is devoted to the Catholic spiritual understanding of dying and to the sacraments and rites that accompany the death of a Catholic. Taken together, the two parts can improve the reader's understanding of how to die well.

PART I
MORALITY

I

Medically Assisted Nutrition

I first met Mark three years after that terrible day. School had just ended and he was the passenger in a car driven by his friend. As they waited for the light to turn green, catastrophe was barreling full force toward them. A drunk driver fleeing from police slammed into the car, killing Josh and leaving Mark with a severe traumatic brain injury. He survived but with markedly diminished mental capacities. Confined either to his bed or a motorized wheelchair, Mark could not speak; he could not follow simple requests. While his eyes were periodically open, he appeared unaware of his surroundings. At times, however, Mark appeared to react to the voice of his mother and would follow her movements. He could not eat normally. Food and water were supplied by a feeding tube that had been surgically placed through his abdominal wall.

Mark is an example of someone with an impaired level of consciousness. Awareness ranges over a continuum, from fully awake to comatose. A person who is comatose does not open his eyes, even to painful stimulation. This is the lowest level of awareness. Over time, someone in a coma may improve and transition to what is known as a "persistent vegetative state". Someone in a persistent vegetative state may have complex reflexes, including eye movements, yawning, and involuntary reactions to noxious stimuli, but shows no awareness of self or environment. While the term "vegetative" is not meant to be derogatory, the word itself creates an image of a person who is a "vegetable". John Paul II was very critical of this terminology: "A man, even if seriously ill or disabled in the exercise of his highest functions, is and always will be a man, and he will never become a 'vegetable' or an 'animal'."[1] A better term for this condition, which is gaining favor, is "unresponsive wakefulness syndrome".

The minimally conscious state, unlike a vegetative state, is characterized by some evidence of awareness of self and/or the environment. Prognosis for improvement is better for this condition than for unresponsive wakefulness syndrome. Mark seemed to fit this category better as he appeared to respond to his mother's voice. In an attempt to improve Mark's level of awareness even further, I placed electrodes in the part of the brain involved with level of awareness and applied a small amount of electrical current. This therapy is called deep brain stimulation, and it can improve the consciousness of patients in the minimally conscious state, making them more alert and communicative.

The results with Mark were modest: he started to verbalize more and have an awareness of his environment, following movements around him. However, Mark still could not take food or drink by mouth, and he continued to receive nutrition and hydration by his feeding tube. Like many people with severe brain injuries, Mark was susceptible to infections and other medical complications, and ten years after his injury, he passed away.

Mark's story raises many of the questions surrounding medically assisted nutrition and hydration, better known as

---

[1] John Paul II, "Life-Sustaining Treatments and Vegetative State: Scientific Advances and Ethical Dilemmas", Address to the International Congress (March 20, 2004), no 3.

a feeding tube. Mark died of complications associated with his brain injury. He did not die of starvation. Such was not the case with Terri Schiavo. Her case in the 1990s first brought the issue of feeding tubes into the public sphere. Terri was only twenty-six years old when she suffered a cardiac arrest. She was resuscitated but suffered a severe brain injury from lack of oxygen. Despite extensive therapy, Terri never regained consciousness, and her husband asked her physicians to remove a feeding tube that provided her with hydration and nutrition. Terri's parents opposed her husband's decision, and a seven-year legal battle followed. After multiple hearings and appeals at the state and federal levels, the decision to disconnect the feeding tube was ultimately upheld. It took thirteen days for Terri to die. She did not die of her brain injury; she was starved to death.

The Catholic perspective on assisted nutrition and hydration was articulated by Pope John Paul II. In a 2004 speech given to a group of physicians gathered to discuss life-sustaining treatments and the so-called vegetative state, the Holy Father very clearly endorsed the necessity of providing nutrition and hydration to this group of patients:

> I should like particularly to underline how the administration of water and food, even when provided by artificial means, always represents a *natural means* of preserving life, not a *medical act*. Its use, furthermore, should be considered, in principle, *ordinary* and *proportionate*, and as such morally obligatory. . . .
>
> The obligation to provide the "normal care due to the sick in such cases" (Congregation for the Doctrine of the Faith, *Iura et bona*, p. IV) includes, in fact, the use of nutrition and hydration. . . . Death by starvation or dehydration is, in fact, the only possible outcome as a result

of their withdrawal. In this sense it ends up becoming, if done knowingly and willingly, true and proper euthanasia by omission.[2]

Pope Francis has affirmed this teaching by affirming that "required basic care for each person includes the administration of nourishment and fluids needed to maintain bodily homeostasis."[3] Nutrition and hydration do not constitute medical therapy, but are obligatory care. So, the teaching of the Church is clear. For someone who would otherwise continue to live, there is an obligation to provide nutrition and hydration, even if a feeding tube is necessary.

Does that mean that every patient should have a feeding tube placed if he can no longer eat or drink on his own? In short, the answer is no. A feeding tube is not needed for every patient, and in fact, at the end of life, a feeding tube is not required for the majority of patients. How to reconcile this apparent contradiction? According to the U.S. Catholic bishops, "As a patient draws close to inevitable death from an underlying progressive and fatal condition, certain measures to provide nutrition and hydration may become excessively burdensome and therefore not obligatory in light of their very limited ability to prolong life or provide comfort."[4]

In practical terms, for a person who is very near death, the absence of hydration or nutrition does not cause the patient's death. Think, for example, of someone with widely spread, incurable cancer. As the disease progresses, this per-

[2] John Paul II, "Life-Sustaining Treatments", no. 4.
[3] Congregation for the Doctrine of the Faith, letter *Samaritanus bonus* (The Good Samaritan) (June 25, 2020), no. 3.
[4] United States Conference of Catholic Bishops, *Ethical and Religious Directives for Catholic Health Care Services*, 6th ed. (Washington, D.C.: USCCB, 2018), no. 58.

son becomes less alert, less able to eat or drink. Over time, the patient becomes unresponsive and unable to eat or drink anything. Death is very near. In a situation such as this, there is no obligation to place a feeding tube. The person dies of cancer, not starvation or dehydration.

There comes a point when food and water can no longer be assimilated by a dying patient. What does this mean? As death approaches, the body starts to shut down. Organ systems begin to fail. The digestive system no longer works properly. Food is not digested and absorbed. Placing a feeding tube would provide no benefit. If a feeding tube is already in place, and the patient can no longer digest the food, it would be appropriate to stop giving food or even to remove the feeding tube.

Are there other possible exceptions to the obligation to provide assisted nutrition and hydration? Possibly. While there should be a presumption in favor of providing nutrition and hydration, some circumstances may arise that could lead one to reconsider. For example, a comatose patient may regurgitate the tube feedings and suffer from repetitive episodes of aspiration pneumonia. A patient who experiences prolonged periods of uncontrolled agitation may repeatedly pull out the feeding tube, with reinsertion becoming progressively more difficult. In these cases, assisted nutrition might be excessively burdensome.

Those few exceptions aside, we have a duty to provide shelter and food to someone in need of it. A comatose patient should not be left on the sidewalk to die, nor should he be starved to death. The inherent value of human life at all stages and in all degrees of capacity must be protected. As the Congregation for the Doctrine of the Faith explains, "It is always completely false to assume that the vegetative state, and the state of minimal consciousness . . . are signs that the patient has ceased to be a human person with all of the dignity belonging to persons as such. On the contrary, in these states of greatest weakness, the person must be acknowledged in their intrinsic value and assisted with suitable care."[5]

---

[5] Congregation for the Doctrine of Faith, *Samaritanus bonus*, no. 8.

2

Withdrawing Care

It was March, nearing the end of Lent. In the exam room, an elderly woman sat in a wheelchair with a placid, content look on her face. She was accompanied by her family, two daughters and a son, whose concerned countenance betrayed their underlying fears. Mary had been having problems walking, something new for her. Her family doctor had ordered an MRI of her brain, which revealed a large tumor. The next day, Mary arrived in my neurosurgery clinic.

A review of the scan demonstrated a large tumor that could not be safely removed. Almost certainly it was a cancerous, rapidly growing tumor. I recommended a biopsy of the tumor, which was performed a few days later. The biopsy specimen was sent off for analysis, a process that takes several days.

The following week, Mary and her family returned to my office to discuss the biopsy results. As expected, the tumor was a glioblastoma, highly malignant and universally—that is, without exception—fatal. I began our conversation by saying, "Mary, I'm sure it must have been difficult this past week as you waited for the biopsy results."

With the gentlest of smiles, Mary replied: "Oh, Dr. Doran . . . not at all. This has been my holy week." As tears streamed down the faces of her children, Mary and I talked about her prognosis and treatment options. Radiation and chemotherapy were recommended, and appointments with the appropriate specialists arranged. We ended with prayer. Mary tolerated treatment well. First radiation, then chemo. Radiation therapy was not painful, but it was exhausting for Mary to bundle up, drive across town, sit in the waiting room, and lie on the cold table as the quiet whir of the linear accelerator showered electrons on the tumor and the surrounding brain. Five days per week for four weeks. Twenty treatments. Twenty mini-pilgrimages on the road toward death.

As hoped, radiation shrank the tumor; chemotherapy came next. Fortunately, for Mary's tumor, the standard treatment was an oral chemotherapy agent that is usually well tolerated with minimal side effects. Mary took this pill until the inevitable occurred: the glioblastoma started to grow again. She was presented with the option to move on to the next line of treatment: combination chemotherapy delivered intravenously. A port would be needed. Side effects are much more common and much more severe with this treatment. At best, this second line of treatment would extend her life a few more months. Mary thought and prayed and decided enough was enough. No more treatment. She died a couple months later.

Essential to medical decision-making at the end of life is an understanding of the medical conditions present: What is the diagnosis? What is the prognosis? What is the effectiveness of the proposed treatment? What are the side effects associated with treatment? What are the alternative treatments? What would happen if treatment were withheld or withdrawn? (Keep in mind there is no moral distinction between withholding and withdrawing treatment.)

There is a general obligation to maintain health and life, but as the end of life approaches, one can (and should) legitimately ask if treatment should begin or continue. As modern medicine progressed during the twentieth century, this question became more prevalent, and Pope Pius XII addressed it in 1957:

> Natural reason and Christian morals say that man (and whoever is entrusted with the task of taking care of his fellowman) has the right and the duty in case of serious illness to take the necessary treatment for the preservation of life and health. . . . But normally one is held to use only ordinary means—according to circumstances of persons, places, times, and culture—that is to say, means that do not involve any grave burden for oneself or another.[1]

Pope Pius highlighted the important distinction between treatment that is ordinary and treatment that is extraordinary. Other authors have used the terms *proportionate* versus *disproportionate*. Proportionate treatment is, in the judgment of the patient (or, if he is mentally incapacitated, his authorized caregiver), treatment that gives reasonable hope of benefit without excessive burden or expense for family or community.[2] The question at hand is whether a given treatment presents a "grave burden" to the patient or caregivers. It is important to realize that there is not a "list" of treatments that can be cleanly divided into ordinary and extraordinary.

Many factors must be considered before determining whether a treatment is overly burdensome. The patient's own assessment of how burdensome the treatment in question

---

[1] Pius XII, "The Prolongation of Life", address to the International Congress of Anesthesiologists, November 24, 1957, reprinted in *National Catholic Bioethics Quarterly* (Summer 2009): 327–32.

[2] United States Conference of Catholic Bishops, *Ethical and Religious Directives for Catholic Health Care Services*, 6th ed. (Washington, D.C.: USCCB, 2018), no. 56.

would be is most important, as it is the patient who will have to endure the treatment and its side effects.

Pain is experienced at multiple levels (physical, emotional, and spiritual), every person varies in his level of tolerance for pain, and the same treatment can create different amounts of pain. Mary judged that biopsy, radiation, and the first kind of chemotherapy were not overly burdensome and would roughly double the amount of time she had left to live. While the diagnosis and subsequent treatments caused some degree of pain and suffering, in Mary's judgment the suffering was balanced by extending her life, giving her time to be with family. She believed her suffering was redemptive, and she put it to good use.

Let's consider another example on the other end of the spectrum. That is, some patients desire to receive any and all available treatments, even when the chances of recovery or cure are remote. Even the most extreme measures are not seen as burdensome. Roberta was the mother of four boys when she first was diagnosed with breast cancer. I first met Roberta when she was forty-one years old, about ten years after her initial diagnosis. Her speech was slurred, and her handwriting had deteriorated; an MRI revealed spread of the breast cancer to her cerebellum, the portion of the brain responsible for coordination. Removing the single metastasis was a relatively low-risk surgery, and the benefits for her long-term survival were significant. Like most patients in this situation, Roberta consented to surgery, which was followed by radiation therapy.

Three years later, she developed a recurrent tumor in the same vicinity. Repeat surgery was more risky and less likely to help her long-term prognosis. Once again, Roberta desired to have surgery. As expected, her recovery was more difficult and, unfortunately, within a short time, the cancer had spread throughout her entire nervous system, covering the surface of the brain and the spinal cord with a coating of tumor cells. Her prognosis was dismal, and survival beyond a few months was not expected. In my experience, most patients in similar situations would be hesitant to undergo further treatments, especially if painful or invasive. Bobbi was different; she wanted to continue any available treatment.

She became bedridden from lower-extremity paralysis. Her bladder stopped working, necessitating placement of a permanent catheter. Yet, she and her husband made the heroic effort for her to receive daily radiation treatments, even as her condition continued to deteriorate. In a last-ditch effort, her oncologist recommended chemotherapy infused directly into the fluid spaces deep within the brain via a surgically placed reservoir. I saw Roberta for the last time in pre-op. I had mixed thoughts about the surgical procedure about to follow. Everyone—Roberta, her husband, her oncologist, and I—knew that this would at best prolong her survival by weeks or a few short months. By most accounts, this was burdensome treatment: painful, invasive, not likely to help much. Yet Bobbi did not see things this way. Just before surgery, we prayed briefly and I said to her, "Bobbi, you know you don't have to do this." She smiled faintly and nodded, "I know." I asked, "What makes you continue to try so hard?" Her response: "For my family."

Each of these examples illustrates that a patient's personal experience determines whether a given treatment is overly burdensome. You could say it is in the eye of the beholder. The same treatment for the same condition may or may not be extraordinary or disproportionate. As mentioned above, there is an obligation to preserve life, but as Pius XII said, whether a given treatment is burdensome depends upon the circumstances of persons, places, times, and cultures. Mary's and Roberta's stories highlight this reality.

As conditions change, a patient's experience of what is or is not burdensome can also change. Initially, a given treatment may be ordinary or proportionate, but with progression of the underlying condition, continued treatment may become extraordinary or disproportionate. The ratio between benefits and risks can shift over time. Mary's story helps illustrate this point. Initially, it made sense to treat the glioblastoma. There was a reasonable probability that she would respond to the treatment, and despite the risks and pain associated with the biopsy, radiation, and chemotherapy, she consented to treatment. However, when the tumor started to grow again, continued treatment that was more invasive and more likely to cause burdensome side effects shifted the ratio between risks and benefits, and Mary decided to stop treating the brain cancer.

Ventilators

Tim was in the prime of his life. He was blessed with a loving wife, three healthy kids, and a blossoming career. But then, truly out of the blue, Tim was found lying on the sidewalk, barely breathing. Paramedics arrived within a few minutes and placed a breathing tube. Upon arrival at the hospital, a CT revealed a massive stroke on the left side of Tim's brain. He was whisked to the neuro-interventional suite, where a catheter from the femoral artery in his groin to the middle cerebral artery in his brain was inserted. Next a clot-busting device was used to break up the thrombus lodged in the blood vessel feeding the left side of his brain. While the procedure went as well as expected, restoring flow to the brain did not reverse the effects of the stroke. Within forty-eight hours, Tim's brain began to swell, so I surgically removed a large portion of his skull to make room for his brain to expand so that pressure would decline. In spite of all these and other efforts, Tim declined even further. Survival was highly improbable, and even if he were to live, he would never again be independent. His speech functions were lost forever. With such a grim prognosis, Tim's family requested that the ventilator be stopped and the breathing tube removed. Surrounded by his wife and children, Tim died within a couple of hours.

The decision to stop treatment is never easy, and some situations are so complicated that this decision is even harder to make. One such situation is when the patient is incapacitated and unable to make decisions for himself. From a moral perspective, there is not a distinction between initially refusing a ventilator and removing the ventilator. However, it often doesn't seem that way for the person tasked with making these decisions for someone else. Often, the decision to resuscitate and place a patient on a ventilator is made in the heat of the moment. The decision to remove the ventilator, on the other hand, requires emotionally difficult deliberation.

Almost every week, I am confronted with this situation: Someone is found unresponsive at home. EMS is called and the patient is intubated (a breathing tube is placed). Upon arrival at the ER, a CT reveals a massive, inoperable brain bleed, and the patient is transferred to the ICU. Within a few days, it is clear that the patient will not survive, or if he does survive, severe permanent neurologic injury is inevitable. Continued care in the ICU *may* be burdensome, and stopping life support *may* be the appropriate decision. Notice that a blanket statement cannot be made.

Many factors need to be considered before deciding that
continued care is extraordinary or disproportionate: How
severe is the brain damage? What are the medical conditions
that might inhibit recovery? How old is the patient? And so
on. At some point, the benefits to the patient are eclipsed by
the burdens, and after prayerful discernment, the decision
can be made to withdraw life support and allow the patient
to die.

Decisions to withhold or withdraw a ventilator or similar life-support measures require an understanding of the
underlying medical condition *and* of the desires of the patient, which hopefully have been discussed in advance. If a
patient's condition is so critical that he is on life support,
communication is difficult, if not impossible. The decision
to withhold or to withdraw a ventilator highlights the importance of prayerful preparation for such an event. While
advance directives are covered in more detail elsewhere, it is
helpful now to see how these documents are used. Two legal forms often included with advance directives are a living
will and durable power of attorney for health care. Durable
power of attorney for health care is given to a surrogate, who
then makes medical decisions for the incapacitated patient.
A living will typically includes instructions regarding what
type of care a person desires or does not desire at the end of
life, and it will sometimes include blanket statements pro-
hibiting life support under certain circumstances. However,
it is impossible to predict in advance all the possible scenarios in which the use of a ventilator would be ordinary or
extraordinary care. Thus, living wills are discouraged, while
having a designated surrogate faithful to Catholic teaching
is highly encouraged.

In my experience, sometimes people have a misplaced
sense of responsibility. By deciding to stop life support, they

feel as if they are somehow causing the death of their loved one: "If I tell you to pull the plug, I'm telling you to kill my spouse." In situations like this, I try gently to inform the decision maker that the massive brain hemorrhage is causing the death of his loved one and that the ventilator was a tool that helped us while we figured out what was going on. By removing life support, we are allowing things to run their normal course and allowing the patient to die from natural causes. However, while the mind can agree with this statement, the heart may not immediately follow. It may take some time before the decision maker is emotionally ready to stop life support, and the person must not be made to feel coerced.

3

Palliative Care, Hospice, and Pain Control at the End of Life

Life was pretty straightforward for Zach. Wake up at 6 A.M.; head to the welding shop; get off at 5 P.M. and have a few beers with the boys; head home and watch Netflix. On weekends, a few beers typically turned into a few more. Maybe throw in some weed for good measure, unless it was his weekend with Kaylie. Then he would stay sober. He lived for those weekends. Separated but not divorced from Janel, Zach was able to keep it together enough so that he did not lose joint custody of their daughter, and he was able to maintain some semblance of a terse but workable relationship with Janel.

Zach kept his hair shaved close. His neck was adorned with a tattoo that was an artist's rendition of the underlying musculature and blood vessels. Imagine the skin from his chin to his collarbone peeled off; that is what it looked like. Unless he wore a turtleneck sweater (which of course would never happen), the tattoo was always on display and impossible to ignore. The nearly bald head, sinewy physique, and garish tattoo effectively said, "Don't mess with me." He had zero interest in anything having to do with God.

He could ignore it for a few months, but after a while the lump in his right testicle became uncomfortably large, and he reluctantly saw a doctor. He was uninsured and hated hospitals. Within short order, the cancerous testicle was

removed, a port placed in his chest, and chemotherapy initiated. Unfortunately, things did not go as planned. The port
became infected and was removed. Chemotherapy was in-
terrupted, and Zach was poorly compliant with his oncologist's recommendations. In frustration, the oncologist told
Zach he would no longer see him as a patient, and Zach did
nothing about the disease for about six months.

The cancer returned with a vengeance. Unable to toler-
ate the pain and fatigue, Zach reluctantly went to the ER,
where widely metastatic disease was diagnosed. A cure by
this time was improbable at best. Things went from bad to
worse. Zach was again poorly compliant with his treatment,
failing to keep scheduled imaging appointments, skipping
chemotherapy infusions, and leaving the hospital against
medical advice. As his pain and disability worsened, palliative care professionals were consulted to assist with pain
control, behavioral counseling, and management of complicated social dynamics. Zach could no longer work. He went
into increasing debt. Time with his beloved Kaylie dwindled
to almost nothing. He became increasingly despondent and
threatened to kill himself on more than one occasion.

The surging tide of cancer overwhelmed Zach. It spread to
his brain, and surgery was performed to remove a large mass
that was causing him to lose vision. Radiation followed, and
his condition stabilized for a few weeks. He had frequent
telehealth visits with the palliative care team, whose physicians, nurses, and social workers did their best to help Zach,
although he often rebuffed their efforts. Salvage chemotherapy continued, but any gains were short-lived. He required
enormous doses of morphine and oxycodone to keep his
pain at least bearable. Narcan, an opioid-reversing medication, was always nearby. With increasing doses of narcotics,
patients become tolerant to the pain-relieving properties of

these medications, and they need higher and higher doses to achieve the same degree of pain control. However, tolerance does not develop to the respiratory depression that occurs with high-dose narcotics, and Narcan can pull patients away from the precipice of an overdose, accidental or intentional.

Zach's final hospitalization occurred when he abruptly lost the ability to walk. Metastatic testicular cancer invaded his spinal canal, compressing the spinal cord at his upper thoracic spine, causing excruciating pain at the level of the tumor and total paralysis and numbness from the neck down. Palliative radiation was given to help lessen the pain, with the understanding that Zach would never walk again and would forever lose control of his bowel and bladder function.

Once the radiation was completed, Zach transitioned from palliative care to hospice care. His living situation was not stable enough for him to go home, so he was placed in a hospice care center where he lived his final few weeks. Pain control and alertness were not always achievable simultaneously. In his final days, Zach could initially endure a few hours of wakefulness, but as the cancer progressed, he could withstand only a few moments of being alert before the pain became excruciating, and opioids and other medications were infused to bring relief. Zach's final breath came a few moments after his final dose of morphine.

Zach's case sheds light on several issues associated with dying and death: palliative care, hospice care, and pain control at the end of life. His medical care was complicated, but his social situation made things even more challenging. Medical care at all times, but especially during the process of dying, ought to encompass care for the whole person, including his medical, social, emotional, and spiritual needs.

The word "palliative" comes from the Latin *palliare*,

meaning "to cloak". According to the World Health Organization, "Palliative care is an approach that improves the quality of life of patients (adults and children) and their families who are facing problems associated with life-threatening illness. It prevents and relieves suffering through the early identification, correct assessment and treatment of pain and other problems, whether physical, psychosocial or spiritual."[1] While receiving palliative care, patients can still receive medical treatment intended to cure or to control underlying illness. The majority of patients in need of palliative care suffer from chronic illnesses, such as cancer, cardiovascular disease, chronic respiratory diseases, kidney failure, and neurological conditions such as Parkinson's disease, multiple sclerosis, and dementia. Palliative care is not dependent on the patient's prognosis and should be distinguished from hospice, which delivers palliative care at the end of life.[2] When the disease progresses to the point where it is no longer treatable, or if the patient decides to forgo additional treatment, palliative care gives way to hospice care. Attempts to cure any diseases are stopped.

Hospice care and palliative care are often confused with each other, as they share similar goals of symptom relief. However, they are distinct in a number of important ways, and thus will be considered separately. The recognition of palliative care as a specific type of medical care is a more recent development, while the history of hospice care extends back many centuries. The word *hospice* derives from Latin *hospitum*, meaning "hospitality" or "place of rest and protec-

[1] "Palliative Care", World Health Organization, August 5, 2020, who.int/n ews-room/fact-sheets/detail/palliative-care.

[2] Suzanne Gross and Marie Hilliard, "Palliative Care, Pain Management, and Human Suffering", in *Catholic Health Care Ethics: A Manual for Practitioners*, 2nd ed. (Philadelphia: National Catholic Bioethics Center, 2009), 193.

tion for the ill and weary". Historians believe the first hospices originated in Malta around 1065 and were dedicated to caring for the ill and the dying traveling to and from the Holy Land. In the early fourteenth century, the order of the Knights Hospitaller of Saint John of Jerusalem opened the first hospice in Rhodes.[3]

The origin of modern-day hospice care is credited to Cicely Saunders, a twentieth-century British nurse and social worker who devoted her professional life to the care of terminally ill patients. She initially volunteered in the St Luke's Home for the Dying Poor in England. Her experiences led her to obtain a medical degree in 1957.[4] Recognizing the unmet needs of dying patients in hospitals, she established St Christopher's Hospice and developed a comprehensive approach to dealing with the variety of symptoms and suffering often experienced by patients with progressive debilitating disease.

Saunders explained hospice as a philosophy of care that understands pain as not only physical, but also experienced as spiritual and psychological suffering. In the United States, hospice care is delivered in hospitals, skilled nursing facilities, specialized hospice centers, and private homes. About half of all hospice patients receive care in the home by family members who are guided by a hospice team consisting of the patient's personal physician, a hospice physician, social workers, nurses, nurses' aides, trained volunteers, and clergy or other spiritual counselors.

An important consideration is that hospice care is a covered Medicare benefit. However, in order to be eligible for hospice care, a patient must be certified by a physician as

---

[3] Stephen Lutz, "The History of Hospice and Palliative Care", *Current Problems in Cancer* 35, no. 6 (December 2011), 304.

[4] Lutz, "History of Hospice", 305.

terminally ill, which according to the Social Security Act, means the patient has a life expectancy of six months or less. In addition, the patient must be willing to forgo curative treatment.[5] This requirement is what especially distinguishes hospice care from palliative care.

Ethical Concerns at the End of Life

There are a number of ethical concerns as the end of life approaches: assisted hydration and nutrition, pain control, and palliative sedation. Assisted nutrition is covered in more detail in chapter 1, but in brief, medically assisted hydration and nutrition are typically administered through a feeding tube placed in the stomach or small intestine. In general, patients with an existing feeding tube who are admitted to hospice care can continue to receive medically assisted hydration and nutrition until it becomes overly burdensome and disproportionate care. Typically, new feeding tubes are not placed once a patient is enrolled in hospice care. This might be a deterrent to some patients and families, as the underlying principle guiding medical decision-making is that it is not the withholding of nutrition and hydration that should be the cause of death, but the underlying illness. A patient should not die of dehydration or starvation.

One of the fears of a terminally ill patient and family members is uncontrolled pain. No one wants to experience pain, and no one wants to witness it. Pain in all its forms (physical, psychological, spiritual) is present to greater or lesser degrees in all dying patients, and all attempts should

[5] Carolyn Laabs, "Hospice Care", in *Catholic Health Care Ethics: A Manual for Practitioners*, 3rd ed. (Philadelphia: National Catholic Bioethics Center, 2020), 213.

be made to bring relief for all pain, not just physical pain. However, physical pain is particularly feared. In my practice as a neurosurgeon, I diagnose and treat patients with malignant brain tumors, many of which are universally fatal within a year or two. The conversation with patients and their families follows a typical pattern: They want to know the diagnosis, the treatment options, the prognosis. After the facts are gathered, there is a pause in the conversation and the patient or family member asks quietly, "What will it be like in the end? Will it be painful?" In the case of malignant brain tumors, the answer is "No, it usually is not very painful, and if there is pain, it can usually be easily controlled." But not all terminal diseases end the same way. Some cancers can create tremendous amounts of pain as the malignancy infiltrates bones or internal organs. Other terminal diseases, both cancerous and noncancerous, create other types of pain: for example, air hunger in the patient with terminal emphysema and intractable nausea with metastatic tumors of the digestive system.

The Principle of Double Effect
and Pain Control at the End of Life

Hospice and palliative care specialists maintain that in the majority of situations, pain in its various forms can usually be controlled at the end of life with appropriate medications, and these medications do not hasten death. In a relatively small number of cases, large doses of pain medications are needed to control pain, but these large doses may suppress the patient's ability to breathe, and death is hastened. Is that permissible? How is this different from "mercy killing" or euthanasia? The intent of the patient and treating physician is an important factor in distinguishing euthanasia from morally acceptable yet potentially death-hastening pain treatment. An examination of the elements of a good versus an evil act will help us understand better.

According to the *Catechism of the Catholic Church*, the morality of a given action depends on the following: (1) the object chosen, (2) the end in view or the intention, and (3) the circumstances of the action.[6] These are called the moral determinants of an action. The object chosen is the action itself. For a given action to be morally acceptable, the action itself must be morally good or at least neutral. The object of the act is outside the person and is perceivable to others.

The intention of a person can determine whether a particular action is good. For example, mowing your neighbor's lawn with the intention of helping your neighbor as inspired by love for God is much different from mowing your neighbor's lawn to obtain some favor in return. The intent is within the person. Unlike the object of the action, the intent is not directly perceivable by others.

The action and the intention are the primary elements of a moral act, while the circumstances are secondary. They can either increase or decrease the moral goodness or evil of a particular act, and they can also diminish or increase the person's responsibility. Some actions, such as torture or murder, are always wrong, regardless of the intention of the person or surrounding circumstances. A morally good act requires the goodness of its object, of its end, and of its circumstances together.

The principle of double effect helps guide decision-making on many moral issues, especially those surrounding pain con-

---

[6] *Catechism of the Catholic Church* [hereafter cited as *CCC*]: 1750–61.

trol at the end of life. According to this principle, if certain conditions are met, someone can perform an action that is intended to produce a good effect, yet an anticipated but unintended bad effect occurs at the same time. For example, a gangrenous leg of a diabetic patient is amputated; the life of the patient is saved (a good effect) but the ability to walk is severely impaired (a bad effect). This example is fairly simple and straightforward, but the double effect principle can help guide medical decision-making in more complicated, difficult cases.

Four conditions govern this principle. First, the action itself must be morally good or at the very least morally indifferent, neither good nor bad. Second, only the good effect of the action must be intended; the bad effect, while foreseen, must not be intended. Third, the good effect must not occur by means of the bad effect; that is, the end does not justify the means. Finally, there must be a proportionately grave reason to permit the bad effect.

The double effect principle can be applied when treating the pain of terminally ill patients. The good effect is pain control, and the bad effect is the suppression of breathing and the hastening of death. The four conditions are met because (1) the use of morphine or other pain medications is neither good nor bad in itself, (2) administering the morphine is intended only to relieve pain and not to cause death by respiratory depression, (3) morphine provides pain relief by binding to certain pain receptors in the nervous system; the death of the patient is not the means by which morphine works to relieve pain, and (4) the relief of pain is a proportionately grave reason for tolerating the hastening of death.

Thus, the principle of double effect allows for the moral use of pain medications that may hasten death (assuming a proportionately grave reason). However, if the double effect principle is applied to physician-assisted suicide, the opposite conclusion is reached. In this case, as we examine the four conditions for the principle, we see that the first condition is met: the use of morphine is morally neutral. However, the second condition is not met: the intent of giving the morphine or other medications is primarily to hasten death, not to relieve pain. The third condition is also violated: the morphine is the means by which the patient dies. The fourth condition does not apply because the violation of the second and third conditions shows that the death of the patient is not an unintended but permitted side effect at all, but the intent of the action. As can be seen, the conditions of the double effect principle are not met with assisted suicide, so this principle cannot be used to justify the action.

A related but distinct moral concern at the end of life is the use of palliative sedation, also known as terminal sedation. In some situations, as the end of life approaches, medications are used to sedate a patient who is experiencing suffering that cannot be relieved in any other way. While pain medications are given with the intent of relieving pain, the sedation that can simultaneously occur is not the reason these medications are given. On the other hand, medications can also be given with the intention of causing sedation— they are meant to deprive the patient of consciousness. The double effect principle may apply in some such cases, but terminal sedation is one step closer to assisted suicide and has the potential to be abused. Suffering is experienced at multiple levels (physical, psychological, emotional, etc.), so the goals of terminal sedation must be very specific and used only when the patient is imminently dying and experiencing suffering that is refractory, or resistant, to standard treatments. Care must be taken that the sedation is not the direct cause of death. According to the *Ethical and Religious Directives for Health Care Services*,

> Patients should be kept as free of pain as possible so that they may die comfortably and with dignity, and in the place where they wish to die. Since a person has a right to prepare for his or her death while fully conscious, he or she should not be deprived of consciousness without a compelling reason. Medicines capable of alleviating or suppressing pain may be given to a dying person, even if this therapy may indirectly shorten the person's life so long as the intent is not to hasten death. Patients experiencing suffering that cannot be alleviated should be helped to appreciate the Christian understanding of redemptive suffering.[7]

[7] United States Conference of Catholic Bishops, *Ethical and Religious Directives for Catholic Health Care Services*, 6th ed. (Washington, D.C.: USCCB, 2018), no. 61.

4

Advance Directives

Anna was only in her fifties, young by most people's standards. She and her husband, Paul, had two teenage children, both enrolled at their respective all-girls and all-boys Catholic high schools. Once the kids were in school full-time, she had returned to work as a hospital nurse. Paul was in management with a national telecommunications company. Life was good. Until it wasn't.

Lurking in Anna's brain was a large aneurysm just behind her left eye. She had no symptoms, no warning. Then she had what is described as a "thunderclap headache": the most sudden, severe pain from out of nowhere. The aneurysm had burst and was flooding her brain with blood. She was at home making dinner and fell to the ground. For a brief time, she was conscious, able to tell Paul what had just happened. She quickly became unresponsive. The paramedics arrived in about ten minutes, intubated her, and brought her to the closest hospital.

When I met Anna in the ICU, she had a score of three, the worst possible score, on the Glasgow Coma Scale. No eye-opening. No response to pain. No verbalization. The large amount of blood that had poured out of the ruptured aneurysm had created a blockage of the normal spinal fluid circulation. Anna developed acute hydrocephalus, severe enlargement of the ventricles, the spinal fluid chambers of the brain. As the ventricles enlarged, pressure inside the brain

47

increased. Without emergent treatment, Anna's brain would herniate, and she would quickly die.

I joined Paul in the waiting room. Unlike many couples in their age group, Paul and Anna had had a number of conversations over the years about what type of treatment they would be willing to accept. Paul knew that Anna would want maximal treatment if it had a reasonable chance of success. I explained to Paul that I could treat the hydrocephalus by placing an external ventricular drain: an incision is made followed by drilling a small hole in the skull through which a flexible tube is inserted into the ventricle, allowing spinal fluid to drain and pressure to be relieved. The risks of the procedure are relatively low, and it could save Anna's life. Paul consented, and I placed the drain at Anna's bedside in the ICU.

With the pressure relieved, Anna's condition improved slightly, but only for a short period of time. After the drain was placed, she would open her eyes and withdraw her arms and legs in response to painful stimuli. Her Glasgow Coma Scale number improved to seven, but she was still comatose. Surgery was scheduled for the following morning. About an hour beforehand, Anna's aneurysm ruptured again. She "blew a pupil"—that is, her left pupil became massively dilated, an indication that despite the drainage of spinal fluid, pressure had rapidly increased, and swelling was causing her brain to herniate. A CT scan confirmed that the large hemorrhage was now massive. A surgery that was difficult to begin with now became exponentially riskier. At best, clipping the aneurysm would prevent further hemorrhage; at worst, surgery would exacerbate the swelling and Anna would die.

Paul and I met again. The second hemorrhage made a bad situation much worse. Even if Anna survived, she would likely never regain consciousness. What is the decision?

Surgery or no? Anna could not decide for herself; Paul had to decide for her. And he knew what she would want now. They had talked about it; they had it written down in an advance directive. If further treatment had minimal chance of success, then she would not want it. No surgery. A few days later, Anna died.

Anyone who checks in to the hospital is asked a series of questions: Can I see some identification? Do you have your insurance card? Do you have a copy of your advance directive? Most people can easily address the first two questions, while the third question may not be as easily answered. Some patients come prepared with a copy of an advance directive; others have some vague memory of preparing one in the past but did not anticipate ever needing it; some have no idea what is meant by an advance directive. What exactly is an advance directive? Is it really necessary? These are important questions that this chapter will address.

In a nutshell, an advance directive is a legal document that allows patients to communicate their desires for medical treatment in the event that they lose the ability to make decisions for themselves. Typically, the document identifies a surrogate decision maker in the event of incapacity. As long as a patient remains conscious and mentally competent, medical decisions generally remain at the discretion of the patient. However, as a result of a serious illness or sudden injury, a person may no longer be capable of making decisions, and an advance directive serves as a template for others to make those decisions on his behalf. Advance directives have become commonplace in response to the Patient Self-Determination Act of 1990, which requires health-care providers to inform patients of their rights under state law to make decisions concerning their medical care, inquire as to whether a patient has executed an advance directive, and document the patient's wishes regarding their medical care.

Two forms are often included in an advance directive: (1) a durable power of attorney for health care and (2) a living will. A third document is becoming increasingly common, namely Physician Orders for Life-Sustaining Treatment (POLST). Don't let the legalese deter you from reading further. While I would argue that lifelong, spiritual preparation for death is far and away the most important element of the art of dying, end-of-life decision-making is not to be ignored. An advance directive ought to be prepared in conversation with family (or close friends) who know you well *and* are faithful to the teachings of the Catholic Church. As we will see later, the unintended consequences of a poorly worded living will or POLST could encourage your surrogate to make a decision that is not in line with Catholic moral teaching.

A few details are in order before going further. Advance directives become legal documents when they are signed by the person named on the document. A lawyer is not needed to complete the forms, but the signature must be witnessed and sometimes notarized, depending on state law. The person completing the advance directive must be of legal age, usually eighteen years old, and must freely express the desire to complete it. He must be free of any coercion and must be mentally competent to comprehend and communicate medical decisions. An advance directive can be revised at any time and is generally valid across state lines.

The most important document, and arguably the only document needed, in an advance directive is durable power of attorney for health care. This is a legal document that authorizes another person (known as a surrogate) to make medical decisions for someone who is not able to make decisions for himself. When a person is critically ill or injured, often he is not able to make decisions and communicate them to physicians and nurses. In certain situations, the patient might be sedated while on a ventilator. Sometimes a patient is awake and talking but is clearly confused or disoriented and unable to make decisions. A wide range of scenarios exists where a person cannot guide his own medical care and a durable power of attorney for health care identifies someone else to make those decisions. The power to guide medical care might be temporary, such as in cases when the patient regains the ability to make their own decisions, or the power might continue until death, if the patient never regains the ability to make decisions.

When choosing someone to act as your medical decision maker, you should have a conversation with that person, or better yet, an ongoing discussion with him. Keep in mind that this surrogate must have an understanding of your medical conditions and treatment options and be willing to follow your desires even if he or she does not agree with them. The most important factor in choosing someone to be your medical decision maker is that person must know your values and preferences for end-of-life decisions.

Ethical and Religious Directives (ERD) by the U.S. bishops is an important document that addresses many topics in medical ethics. It gives specific guidelines pertaining to advance directives and durable powers of medical attorney. The bishops encourage people to make their end-of-life decisions known in advance but remind the faithful that the surrogate decision maker must be faithful to the teachings of the Church: "Each person may identify in advance a representative to make health care decisions as his or her surrogate in the event that the person loses the capacity to make health care decisions. Decisions by the designated surrogate should be faithful to Catholic moral principles and to the person's intentions and values, or if the person's intentions are unknown, to the person's best interests."[1] If you do not appoint someone as your surrogate decision maker, family members should assume that role.

A living will is the second document often included in an advance directive. A living will specifies what treatments you want or do not want at the end of your life. At first glance, this seems like a good idea: after all, the more clearly I make my desires known, the easier it will be for my family. As we shall see, however, the unintended consequences of a living will can create a quandary that actually makes things more complicated than you may have intended.

Typically, a living will authorizes a physician to make a variety of decisions, including the following: (1) administering appropriate measures to sustain life; (2) discontinuing curative treatments; (3) withholding life-sustaining treatments; (4) providing comfort care; (5) issuing a "do not resuscitate" (DNR) order; and (6) withholding or withdrawing medically assisted nutrition or hydration.[2] In some situations, a living will may prohibit the use of treatments that would be considered ordinary and not burdensome to the patient.

It is impossible to predict in advance the medical conditions that will be present in someone who is seriously ill. For example, it might be appropriate to refuse or withdraw the use of a ventilator for someone who is actively dying from a terminal illness. On the other hand, the temporary

---

[1] United States Conference of Catholic Bishops, *Ethical and Religious Directives for Catholic Health Care Services*, 6th ed. (Washington, D.C.: USCCB, 2018), no. 25.

[2] Edward J. Furton, ed., *Catholic Health Care Ethics: A Manual for Practitioners*, 3rd ed. (Philadelphia: The National Catholic Bioethics Center, 2020), 247.

use of a ventilator can be lifesaving for someone who has a potentially curable problem, such as a serious pneumonia. Living wills can become problematic, especially with regard to decisions regarding nutrition and hydration: a living will might unconditionally forbid a feeding tube, a decision that conflicts with Catholic moral teaching. For these reasons, among others, living wills are discouraged.

A POLST goes one step further than a living will. While a living will is a legal document that serves as a guideline for medical decision-making, a POLST is an actual medical order signed by a qualified clinician that authorizes the medical treatment a patient chooses to receive or not receive at the end of life. Just as with living wills, the standard POLST may authorize decisions that conflict with Catholic morals and do so with an even greater level of authority than a living will. A POLST is part of your medical record. For you to receive treatment or have treatment withdrawn, a medical order is necessary. As part of your medical record, a POLST is a series of orders that clinicians are obliged to follow. While intended to protect your ability to make decisions, a POLST actually undermines your ability to make an informed decision.

For any given medical problem, the decision to treat is based upon many factors, including risks, benefits, side effects, and cost. Understanding these factors is necessary to make an informed decision. It is impossible to predict in advance the myriad of medical conditions that might be present when you are seriously ill or even nearing death. Without full knowledge of the nature of the treatments, it is impossible to make an informed decision. A POLST potentially commits you to a course of treatment, or no treatment, before you or your surrogate has a chance to make an informed decision.

Our preparation for death is both spiritual and practical. An advance directive, particularly a durable power of attorney for health care, is an important practical document that you should consider enacting. However, living wills and POLSTs are inherently problematic and should be avoided. The best thing you can do is to identify a surrogate who knows you well, understands your medical conditions, and is willing to uphold your Catholic morals and values in the event that you are unable to speak for yourself.

5

Brain Death

Karla was happy, eager to help, and willing to brighten everyone's day. She had a fondness for children and worked in a day care center with hopes of becoming a pediatric nurse. She had a two-year-old daughter, Genesis, and was pregnant with a boy, whom she planned to name Angel.[1]

Karla was twenty-two years old and twenty-two weeks pregnant when she experienced a sudden, severe headache. She collapsed and never woke up. She was rushed to the hospital and placed on a ventilator. A CT revealed a massive brain hemorrhage that was beyond any surgical intervention. As the pressure inside her head increased, Karla's brain function deteriorated, leading doctors to declare that she was "brain-dead". Yet, baby boy Angel remained alive in her womb.

He was not developed enough to survive outside the womb, so Karla was kept on life support for another fifty-four days while Angel continued to grow.[2] A ventilator delivered oxygen to her lungs; carbon dioxide was sent back

---

[1] "A Mother's Gift: Remembering Karla Perez, Honoring the Life and Legacy She Left Behind", Methodist (hospital website), July 13, 2020, bestcare.org/news/20200713/mothers-gift-remembering-karla-perez-honoring-life-and-legacy-she-left-behind.

[2] Katy Glover, "54 Days after Nebraska Woman Was Declared Brain Dead, Her Son Was Born", *Omaha World-Herald*, May 1, 2015, updated August 21, 2019, omaha.com/livewellnebraska/health/54-days-after-nebraska-woman-was-declared-brain-dead-her-son-was-born/article_a2b40672-975e-5f64-9272-3332724b8976.html.

in return. Karla's heart pumped blood carrying oxygen and nutrients to her body and, by way of the placenta, to Angel's body.

Karla remained stable for almost eight weeks, but when her heart and other organs began to deteriorate, Angel was delivered by cesarean section at thirty weeks, three days, weighing in at just under three pounds. Angel became the world's sixteenth baby to be born alive after somatic support during pregnancy. After he was born, Karla's heart, liver, and kidneys were donated for transplant. Two months later, Angel was released to the care of his grandparents along with his sister, Genesis.

Most people are probably familiar with the term *brain-dead* but are uncertain about what it really means. Is a "brain-dead" person really dead? Karla's case challenges the current medical and legal position that someone who is brain dead *is* dead and serves as a starting point for exploring medical, moral, and philosophical questions about death.

Theological and Historical Background [3]

While alive on earth, human beings are meant to be an indivisible union of body and soul, and the resurrection of the dead hoped for by Christians is the perfect realization of this harmony. Death is the necessary event linking these two states. However, the starting point of the Christian understanding of death is biological. According to Joseph Ratzinger, death is the "physical process of disintegration

[3] The sections "Theological and Historical Background" and "Catholic Magisterial Teaching" were adapted from Stephen E. Doran and Joseph M. Vukov, "Organ Donation and Declaration of Death: Combined Neurologic and Cardiopulmonary Standards", *The Linacre Quarterly* 86, no. 4 (2019):285–96.

which accompanies life. It is felt in sickness and reaches its terminal point in physical dying."[4]

The life of human beings is not subject to their control. They often seek to gain power over their own existence, but this is an exercise in futility, leading ultimately to anger, frustration, and despair. The alternative response to death is to trust the power that actually controls human existence. "And in this second case, the human attitude towards pain, towards the presence of death within living, merges with the attitude we call love."[5] The confrontation with physical death is the confrontation with the basic question of human existence. For the Christian, "physical death is met within the daring of that love which leaves self behind, giving itself to the other."[6] The God who died in the person of Jesus is the source of this love. When Christians die, they die into the death of Christ himself. "Death is vanquished when people die with Christ and into him. This is why the Christian attitude must be opposed to the modern wish for instantaneous death, a wish that would turn death into an extensionless moment and banish from life the claims of the metaphysical."[7]

In the last hundred years, however, the Christian understanding of death has been challenged by technological advances. Prior to the use of mechanical ventilation during the 1920s, the process of dying ended when individuals could no longer breathe on their own and the heartbeat ceased. This is known as the "cardiovascular criteria" for death. To determine death, physicians would feel for the

[4] Joseph Ratzinger, *Eschatology: Death and Eternal Life* (Washington, D.C.: Catholic University of America Press, 1988), 95.

[5] Ratzinger, *Eschatology*, 96.

[6] Ratzinger, *Eschatology*, 95.

[7] Ratzinger, *Eschatology*, 97.

pulse, listen for breathing, hold a mirror before the nose to test for condensation, and look to see if the pupils were fixed.

The sophistication of mechanical ventilation and other means of artificial life support continued to advance, and by the 1950s a human being with severe brain injury could be sustained for up to a few days before the circulatory system failed and the patient ultimately died. In the days preceding circulatory collapse, clinicians also observed the absence of typical signs of neurological function, leading to the development of clinical criteria of death by neurological standards, also known as "brain death".[8] By and large, however, the determination of death by neurological standards had very limited clinical utility, as ultimately circulatory collapse occurred within a few days.

In a singular event that raised questions about the reliability of the cardiovascular standard, the need for neurological criteria for death was pushed to the clinical forefront. In 1967, Christiaan Barnard performed the first successful human heart transplant. Although the patient died eighteen days later, this operation marked the beginning of heart transplantation. Over a hundred additional heart transplants were attempted within the following year. Many of the early failures were attributed to the donor organ deterioration that occurs while waiting a sufficient time after cardiac arrest to ensure that the donor would not spontaneously resuscitate.[9] Barnard's own account of the first heart transplant reveals that he waited about three minutes after the donor

[8] P. Mollaret and M. Goulon, "Le Coma dépassé", Revue Neurologique 101, no. 1 (July 1959): 3–15.

[9] D. Scott Henderson, Death and Donation: Rethinking Brain Death as a Means for Procuring Transplantable Organs (Eugene, Ore.: Pickwick, 2011), 2.

heart stopped beating before proceeding with its removal.[10] Barnard's choice of three minutes, however, raises a question: Is three minutes enough time to declare confidently that the donor is in fact beyond the point of spontaneous resuscitation? Before the possibility of organ donation, "close enough" criteria may have been sufficient to declare death. The possibility of donation, however, creates a pressing need for a more precise standard. The reason stems from the "dead donor rule", which states: "Vital organs which occur singly in the body can be removed only after death, that is from the body of someone who is certainly dead. This requirement is self-evident, since to act otherwise would mean intentionally to cause the death of the donor in disposing of his organs."[11] To abide by the dead donor rule, it is therefore important to know exactly when a patient has died.

The following year, the Harvard Ad Hoc Committee to Study the Problems of the Hopelessly Unconscious Patient convened to propose new diagnostic criteria for determining death. The finished work of the committee was published in the *Journal of the American Medical Association* as "A Definition of Irreversible Coma" and suggested replacing the cardiovascular criterion with a neurological criterion.[12] Over time, the Harvard criterion for determination of brain-death has become widely accepted. Currently, the majority

[10] Christiaan Barnard and Curtis Bill Pepper, *One Life* (Oxford: Macmillan, 1969), 360.

[11] John Paul II, Address to the 18th International Congress of the Transplantation Society (August 29, 200), no. 4.

[12] Ad Hoc Committee of the Harvard Medical School, "A Definition of Irreversible Coma: Report of the Ad Hoc Committee of the Harvard Medical School to Examine the Definition of Brain Death", *JAMA* 205, no. 6 (1968): 337–40.

of transplanted organs come from individuals who were declared "brain-dead".

Catholic Magisterial Teaching

Both John Paul II and Benedict XVI appeared to endorse the concept of brain death. That might make it seem as if the magisterial teaching on brain death is closed. Crucially, however, both John Paul II and Benedict XVI refused to endorse the Harvard criterion without qualification. That means that the magisterial teaching is not as closed as it may first appear to be.

In his address to the International Congress of the Transplantation Society, John Paul II describes death as an event that no scientific technique can directly identify. It is the total disintegration of the integrated whole that is the human being. He describes death as the separation of the soul from the corporeal reality of the human person. Yet John Paul also acknowledges the need for "scientifically secure means of identifying *the biological signs that a person has indeed died*".[13] He states that "the criterion adopted in more recent times for ascertaining the fact of death, namely the *complete* and *irreversible* cessation of all brain activity, if rigorously applied, does not seem to conflict with the essential elements of a sound anthropology."[14] John Paul also notes, however, that the Church does not make technical decisions regarding the definition of death and depends upon science to guide her in how to understand criteria for death. Benedict XVI

[13] John Paul II, Address to the 18th International Congress of the Transplantation Society, no. 4 (emphasis in original).

[14] John Paul II, Address to the 18th International Congress of the Transplantation Society, no. 5 (emphasis in original).

has likewise affirmed the value of organ transplantation and, much like John Paul, gives qualified acceptance of the brain-death criterion: "In an area such as this, in fact, there cannot be the slightest suspicion of arbitration and where certainty has not been attained the principle of precaution must prevail."[15]

It may seem, then, that the magisterial teaching on brain-death is settled. However, it is no small detail that John Paul qualifies his remarks with "does not seem". Like John Paul, Benedict also leaves room for further debate, warning against the slightest suspicion of arbitrariness and underlining the need for certainty in certifying the death of the patient. And indeed, John Paul himself says that the "acquisition of new data can stimulate and refine moral reflection."[16] As new data are acquired regarding the definition of death, further moral reflection is necessary, and the moral certainty John Paul describes may be revisited in light of this new data.

Current Status of Brain Death

A number of non-dissenting Catholics have raised concerns regarding the validity of brain death as a legitimate definition of death.[17] This concern has been echoed by secular medical ethicists.[18] Karla's case, while rare, is not unique; dozens of pregnant women declared "brain-dead" have been

[15] Benedict XVI, Address to the International Congress of the Transplantation Society (November 7, 2008).

[16] John Paul II, "Determining the Moment When Death Occurs", *Origins* 19, no. 32 (January 11, 1990), no. 6.

[17] See, for example, N. Austriaco, "Is the Brain-Dead Patient Really Dead?" *Studia Moralia* 41 (2003): 277–308.

[18] See D. Scott Henderson, *Death and Donation*.

sustained on life support while the baby continued to develop in the womb.[19] Prolonged survival after declaration
of brain death has been documented in many other cases.[20]
One particularly notable case involved a boy who at age four
became brain-dead secondary to meningitis and survived an
additional twenty years with medical support. Subsequent
autopsy revealed a calcified intracranial shell with no recog-
nizable neural elements grossly or microscopically.[21]

There is growing evidence that many patients declared
dead by neurologic criteria actually have a small portion of
the brain that is still functional.[22] The hypothalamus is a
structure in the brain stem involved in a number of functions, including regulation of hormones, fluid balance, blood
pressure, and body temperature. This realization has created
a conundrum for clinicians, as the Universal Declaration
of Death Act (UDDA) requires that the entire brain, including the brainstem, must be irreversibly dead in order to
declare someone dead using neurologic criteria.[23] This has

[19] Majid Esmaeilzadeh et al., "One Life Ends, Another Begins: Management of a Brain-Dead Pregnant Mother—A Systematic Review", *BMC
Medicine 8*, no. 74 (November 2010), link.springer.com/article/10.1186/1741-
7015-8-74.

[20] D. Alan Shewmon, "Recovery from 'Brain Death': A Neurologist's
Apologia", *The Linacre Quarterly 67*, no. 1 (February 1997): 30-96.

[21] S. Repertinger, William P. Fitzgibbons, M. Omojola, and R. Brumback,
"Long Survival Following Bacterial Meningitis-Associated Brain Destruction", *Journal of Child Neurology 21* (July 1, 2006): 591-95.

[22] Michael Nair-Collins, Jesse Northrup, and James Olcese, "Hypothalamic-
Pituitary Function in Brain Death: A Review", *Journal of Intensive Care
Medicine 31*, no. 1 (March 31, 2014): 41-50.

[23] President's Commission for the Study of Ethical Problems in Medicine
and Biomedical and Behavioral Research, *Defining Death: Medical, Legal and
Ethical Issues in the Determination of Death*, July 1981, scholarworks.iupui.edu/
handle/1805/707.

led some groups, including the American Academy for Neurology,[24] to suggest that a functioning hypothalamus should not exclude someone from being declared brain-dead.[25] This proposal smacks of a tremendously oversimplified utilitarianism: a functioning hypothalamus prevents declaration of brain death; the dead donor rule requires a person to be dead before harvesting his organs; therefore exclude the hypothalamus from the definition of death so that harvesting organs appears to be ethical.

So, where do we go from here? Both John Paul II and Benedict XVI have described organ donation as an act of love, but both also caution that before organs are taken, the individual must be unequivocally dead. Brain-death criteria are widely accepted yet with the advent of new technology, both secular and non-dissenting Catholic ethicists have raised legitimate concerns. For now, a Catholic in good conscience may donate his organs, and health-care workers may use these criteria with moral certainty and, as John Paul II has stated, the criteria are a "necessary and sufficient basis for and ethically correct course of action".[26] However, magisterial teaching in this area may need to be refined in the future. There is precedent for refinement of Catholic teaching that should and does occur in the complex areas of bioethics. *Dignitas personae* is an example of how the Church

[24] James A. Russell et al., "Brain Death, the Determination of Brain Death, and Member Guidance for Brain Death Accommodation Requests: AAN Position Statement", *Neurology* 92, no. 5 (January 2019): 228–32.

[25] Ariane Lewis, Richard J. Bonnie, and Thaddeus Pope, "It's Time to Revise the Uniform Determination of Death Act", *Annals of Internal Medicine* 173, no. 1 (July 7, 2020): 143–44.

[26] John Paul II, Address to the 18th International Congress of the Transplantation Society, no. 5.

appropriately updated teachings from *Donum vitae* regarding procreation:

> The Church's Magisterium has frequently intervened to clarify and resolve moral questions in this area. The Instruction *Donum vitae* was particularly significant. And now, twenty years after its publication, it is appropriate to bring it up to date.
>
> The teaching of *Donum vitae* remains completely valid, both with regard to the principles on which it is based and the moral evaluations which it expresses. However, new biomedical technologies which have been introduced in the critical area of human life and the family have given rise to further questions. . . . These new questions require answers.[27]

The issue of brain death is not an esoteric subject of limited interest to most people. New questions arise, and these require answers. The moments of conception and death mark the beginning and end of our earthly existence, so determining when a person has died carries the same weightiness as determining when an individual comes into existence. Just as technology has pushed against the moral boundaries at the beginning of life, so too does technology force us to reassess the ethical issues at the end of life.

[27] Congregation for the Doctrine of the Faith, Instruction on Certain Bioethical Questions *Dignitas personae* (The Dignity of the Person) (September 8, 2008), no. 1.

6

Perinatal Death

Dr. Bonebrake—of course he is an orthopedic surgeon. How could he be anything different? It doesn't take much imagination to envision Dr. Bonebrake inserting a metal rod in a shattered hip, repairing a torn ACL, internally fixating a fractured wrist, and so on. As it turns out, Dr. Bonebrake cares for the smallest of the small, those so tiny their bones are just beginning to form. Dr. Bonebrake is a physician who practices maternal-fetal medicine, also known as perinatology. He watches over high-risk pregnancies, caring for pregnant moms and their precious cargo. To be under his care, either the mother or the baby must be having serious problems. So, each day is filled with emotionally and hormonally charged pregnant women who fear for their own health or the health of their unborn child; in many cases, they fear for both. Unlike most other specialties, Dr. Bonebrake is simultaneously caring for two patients whose welfare is linked together. If you treat the mom, you are treating the baby and vice versa.

A multitude of moral concerns coalesce in this specialty: assisted reproduction, termination of pregnancy, miscarriage, stillbirth, early induction of labor, fatal fetal anomalies, and so on. Even for someone like myself who is comfortable dealing with challenging medical situations, maternal-fetal medicine seems next level: emotionally and spiritually exhausting. Death is always lurking.

A mind-numbing number of definitions are used by clinicians and the government. When a baby dies after conception determines the "type" of death. According to the U.S. Centers for Disease Control, a miscarriage is usually defined as loss of a baby before the twentieth week of pregnancy, and a stillbirth is loss of a baby at or after twenty weeks of pregnancy. An early stillbirth is a fetal death occurring between twenty and twenty-seven completed weeks of pregnancy. A late stillbirth occurs between twenty-eight and thirty-six completed pregnancy weeks. A term stillbirth occurs between thirty-seven or more completed pregnancy weeks.[1] Perinatal death is defined as a death that occurs from twenty-eight weeks or more, and early neonatal death as a death that occurs after birth but when the baby is less than seven days old.

While the Catholic Church affirms the dignity of life from the moment of conception onward, the emotional and spiritual impact of the loss of a pregnancy can increase as the pregnancy progresses, and even how the remains of the deceased child are treated can change as the pregnancy continues.

Of course, not all high-risk pregnancies result in the death of the mother or the baby. In fact, when the medical problem lies with the mother (hypertension, heart disease, diabetes, cancer, etc.), in most situations, Dr. Bonebrake and his colleagues are able to bring the pregnancy to a point where it is safe to deliver the baby. In other situations, despite their best efforts, something wrong either with the mother or the baby leads to the death of the child.

For women who know they are pregnant, about 10 to

---

[1] "What Is Stillbirth?", Centers for Disease Control and Prevention, last reviewed September 29, 2022, cdc.gov/ncbddd/stillbirth/facts.html.

15 percent of pregnancies end in miscarriage. Most miscarriages happen in the first trimester before the twelfth week of pregnancy. But as many as half of all pregnancies may actually end in miscarriage because a miscarriage may happen before a woman knows she is pregnant.[2] After twenty weeks of pregnancy, approximately 1 out of 100 babies will be stillborn, and each year approximately 24,000 babies are stillborn in the United States.[3] Maternal death can happen, but it is much less common (in the United States, approximately 17 maternal deaths occur for every 100,000 live births).[4]

The Health of the Mother

The best thing that can be done for the health of the baby is to keep the mother healthy. In the vast majority of situations where the mother has a health problem, this can be accomplished and the baby grows and is delivered at term (that is, at thirty-six weeks or later). There are some situations where the health of the mother is placed at risk by the pregnancy, and delivery of the baby is the only way to restore the mother's health. Preeclampsia is one such condition. Preeclampsia is a pregnancy complication characterized by high blood pressure and signs of damage to another organ system, most often the liver and kidneys. Preeclampsia usually begins after twenty weeks of pregnancy in women whose blood pressure had been normal.

[2] "Miscarriage", March of Dimes, last reviewed February 2023, marchofdimes.org/complications/miscarriage.aspx.

[3] "Pregnancy and Infant Loss", CDC, Centers for Disease Control and Prevention, last reviewed September 30, 2022, cdc.gov/ncbddd/stillbirth/features/pregnancy-infant-loss.html.

[4] "Maternal Mortality", Centers for Disease Control and Prevention, last reviewed April 20, 2022, cdc.gov/nchs/maternal-mortality/.

Left untreated, preeclampsia can lead to serious—even fatal—complications for both the mother and her baby. The most effective treatment is delivery of the baby. According to Dr. Bonebrake, since preeclampsia usually occurs later in the pregnancy, in the vast majority of situations, the mother can be treated and delivery postponed until the baby reaches the "age of viability", which is when the baby has a good chance of surviving with appropriate care (generally at twenty-four weeks of the pregnancy, although survival rates are improving for even more premature babies).

But what about conditions such as preeclampsia or uterine infection from premature rupture of membranes, where the health of the mother is at grave risk and the baby has not reached the age of viability? Imagine the scenario in which a pregnant mother is critically ill with preeclampsia and the only remaining effective treatment is to deliver the baby, but the baby is less than twenty weeks old and will not survive after delivery. While according to Dr. Bonebrake, this situation is "really, really rare", it does happen, and the parents are faced with two options, both heartbreaking: (1) continue the pregnancy, placing both mother and baby at extremely high risk of dying; (2) deliver the baby, who will not survive, thus allowing the mother to live. Ethicists have described this and similar scenarios as "vital conflicts". They are some of the most morally heart-wrenching cases in health-care ethics, and each case should be assessed individually.

To guide complex moral decision-making, the principle of double effect is often used. While this line of reasoning might seem technical or even esoteric, it is a foundational principle rooted in Catholic philosophy and theology that has also been adopted by secular ethicists. This principle helps evaluate the difficult situation where an action has both good and bad effects. As we saw previously, for an action with bad effects to be morally permissible, four conditions must be fulfilled: (1) the action itself must be good or at least morally neutral; (2) the good effect of the action must be directly intended and any foreseen bad effect tolerated but not directly intended; (3) the bad effect must not be used as a means to achieve the good effect; and (4) the good effect must be proportionate to the bad effect.

The double effect principle can help determine if early induction of labor is permissible in the situations mentioned above (preeclampsia and uterine infection). Induction of labor is morally neutral (condition 1). The death of the premature baby is foreseen but not directly intended, and the intention of the doctor by inducing labor is to cure the underlying condition (condition 2). The good effect of curing the preeclampsia or infection is not caused by the death of the baby (condition 3). The good effect of curing the underlying condition and thus saving the mother's life is proportionate to the loss of the baby (condition 4).

The *Ethical and Religious Directives for Catholic Health Care Services* by the U.S. bishops illustrates how the principle of double effect can be applied in "vital conflicts":

"Operations, treatments, and medications that have as their direct purpose the cure of a proportionately serious pathological condition of a pregnant woman are permitted when they cannot be safely postponed until the unborn child is viable, even if they will result in the death of the unborn child."[5]

---

[5] United States Conference of Catholic Bishops, *Ethical and Religious Directives for Catholic Health Care Services* 6th ed. (Washington, D.C.: United States Conference of Catholic Bishops, 2018), no. 47.

Using the principle of double effect demonstrates that the decision to induce labor (while exceptionally difficult) can be morally acceptable, even knowing the baby will not survive. The question then arises: Cannot the same argument be made about abortion? Is it morally permissible to abort a baby to save the mother's life? The answer is no, abortion is not allowed to save the mother's life. There is an important difference between inducing labor and performing an abortion: abortion is the *direct killing* of an innocent person, which is intrinsically evil. In contrast to early induction of labor, abortion fails to meet at least two of the conditions of the principle of double effect: the action of abortion is morally wrong (condition 1); the good intention of saving the mother's life is brought about by an evil action (condition 3). It is one thing to deliver a baby early and let God and nature take its course; it is another thing altogether to kill intentionally a child in the womb. Not only is direct abortion morally wrong, even as a means to a good end, but many medical experts argue that surgical abortion is never more effective in saving the mother's life than means that are not destructive to the fetus.[6]

Health of the Baby

Sometimes a baby has a condition that is not correctable, such as a genetic disorder. By its nature, a genetic problem cannot be fixed. Down syndrome is a classic example: people born with Down have an extra chromosome, which leads to its scientific name of Trisomy 21, which means babies with

---

[6] See, for example, "Abortion Never Saves a Life", Life Institute, April 11, 2018, thelifeinstitute.net/campaigns/abortion-never-saves-a-life.

Down end up with three chromosomes at position 21 instead of the usual pair.

Some genetic abnormalities, such as Trisomy 13, are not compatible with prolonged life outside the womb. Another example is anencephaly, which causes the development of only minimal brain tissue. Most children with this condition die before birth, and those who do not rarely live more than a few hours or days after birth.[7] It is precisely in situations such as these that Dr. Bonebrake feels he has the most to offer: "Sometimes when it appears that medically we are going to have a bad outcome, we have the opportunity to have the biggest impact just by being present with the family and walking through the process with them."

A buzzword these days in Catholic circles is "accompaniment". What does that really mean and how does it play out in real life? It seems that accompaniment is often construed as walking beside someone with the hope of helping bring about some change. How are we supposed to accompany someone in what appears to be a hopeless, unchangeable situation? How are we supposed to accompany a pregnant mother who has just found out that her unborn child has a fatal condition?

What Dr. Bonebrake brings to the table is the gift of time: spending time with the parents and maybe even the siblings of the baby who is going to die. The earlier the diagnosis is made, the more time he can spend with the family. And even if he only has a few days or hours with the family, it still matters. That gift of time can make all the difference in the world.

---

[7] "Anencephaly", National Center for Advancing Translational Sciences, GARD (Genetic and Rare Diseases Information Center), last updated February 2023, rarediseases.info.nih.gov/diseases/5808/anencephaly.

When confronted with some problem, our initial reaction often is "Make it go away; make it go away as soon as possible and everything will be fine." A pregnant mother carrying a child with a serious or fatal condition might have the same reaction and thus want to terminate the pregnancy. She might think, "Abort this baby. Now." Dr. Bonebrake's first step on the path of accompaniment is a simple request: "Just take a breath. Come back in a few days, and we can talk some more." No judgment. No finger-wagging. No Bible thumping. Just the suggestion of taking a little time. "And you don't have to do anything," he said. "It's between them and God." In his own words, he just needs to get out of the way, allowing for space and time. And the heart begins to soften, and at the next visit the mother says, "Maybe I don't want to terminate." And the next visit, "I don't want to terminate, but I don't think I can keep the baby." And the next visit, "I'm going to keep the baby. This is *my* baby." And while this softening is not universal, it happens more often than you might imagine.

Infant Death and Baptism

If a child is born and not expected to live very long, Baptism should be performed as soon as possible with the parents' permission. While the ordinary ministers of Baptism are bishops, priests, and deacons, "in case of necessity, anyone, even a non-baptized person, with the required intention, can baptize, by using the Trinitarian baptismal formula."[8]

What if the baby has not yet been born? Can the baby be

[8] *CCC* 1256.

baptized while still in the mother's womb? The answer is no. Baptism is a sacrament that, in order to be valid, must be administered by the actual pouring of water upon the person being baptized, while these exact words are said: "I baptize you in the name of the Father, and of the Son, and of the Holy Spirit." Once the child is born, if there is any possibility that the child is still alive, Baptism can be conditionally administered.

So what happens to infants who die before being baptized? Is there hope for their salvation? Beginning in the Middle Ages, the theory of limbo was developed. Limbo was a state or place for unbaptized infants who die. Since unbaptized infants who die are still subject to original sin, went the argument, they can not share in the beatific vision, but at the same time, they are not subjected to any punishment, because they are not guilty of any personal sin. This theory has been largely abandoned and is not mentioned in the current *Catechism of the Catholic Church*.

For infants who die without Baptism, the fundamental principle to consider is God's desire for the salvation of all. This desire is revealed in a divine love that is both universal and preferential. This divine love is realized through Jesus Christ, the unique Savior of all. Sin is universal, as is the need for salvation, and God desires that all of us be saved. However, from the very beginning, the Church has proclaimed the necessity of Baptism for salvation. This appears to create a spiritual Gordian knot: an unborn infant cannot be baptized, a dead infant cannot be baptized, Baptism is needed for salvation. The International Theological Commission's document on the question expresses the problem succinctly: "The question of the eternal destiny of infants who die unbaptized is 'one of the most difficult to solve in the structure of theology'.[9] It is the 'limit-case' where vital tenets of the faith, especially the need for Baptism for salvation and the universal salvific will of God, can easily appear to be in tension."[10]

However, God does not demand the impossible, and God's power is not restricted to the sacraments. "At all times and in all circumstances, God provides a remedy of salvation for humanity."[11] How might we imagine such a remedy? Infants who suffer and die are, in a sense, already conformed to the suffering and death of Christ, whose Resurrection is the source of man's hope. For infants who experience the violent death of abortion, we can easily see a solidarity with the Holy Innocents, who experienced the baptism of blood that brings salvation. Maybe God simply gives the gift of salvation to unbaptized infants in the same way he gave Mary the grace of salvation in Christ at her Immaculate Conception.[12]

Regardless of which remedy God may use, we can have the firm hope for the salvation of infants who die without Baptism. The ordinary way of salvation through Baptism is certain. However,

> there are theological and liturgical reasons to hope that infants who die without Baptism may be saved and brought into eternal happiness, even if there is not an explicit teach-

[9] Y. Congar, *Vaste monde ma paroisse: Vérité et dimensions du Salut* (Paris: Témoignage Chrétien, 1968), 169: "un de ceux dont la solution est la plus difficile ensynthèse théologique".

[10] International Theological Commission, "The Hope of Salvation for Infants Who Die Without Being Baptized", International Theological Commission (April 22, 2007), no. 70.

[11] International Theological Commission, "The Hope of Salvation", no. 83.

[12] International Theological Commission, "The Hope of Salvation", nos. 85–87.

ing on this question found in Revelation. . . . There are reasons to hope that God will save these infants precisely because it was not possible to do for them that what would have been most desirable—to baptize them in the faith of the Church and incorporate them visibly into the Body of Christ.[13]

[13] International Theological Commission, "The Hope of Salvation", no. 1.

7

Euthanasia

Ernie Chambers was a firebrand politician. An unabashed atheist, he served in the Nebraska legislature for forty-six years. Over the years, he repeatedly introduced legislation to legalize physician-assisted suicide. Fortunately, these bills never saw the light of day, dying in committee every time they were introduced. Near the end of his career, he made a final attempt, and I traveled to Lincoln to testify against the bill. Known for his brash words and proclivity for browbeating anyone who opposed him, Ernie stared down the audience in the legislative chambers, wagged his finger, and said, "There is nothing good about suffering. There is nothing redemptive about suffering." And truth be told, from the perspective of an atheist, his argument holds water: suffering is meaningless; nothing good comes from suffering. It is the age-old argument against the existence of God. Why would an all-loving God allow suffering to exist?

"Put it out of its misery." So many times we may have heard that phrase used to justify the killing of a sick or injured animal. The critically acclaimed movie *They Shoot Horses, Don't They?* (1969) centers precisely on this proposal. As the movie begins, Robert, the leading male character, recalls when a horse with a broken leg was shot to end its misery. The movie tells the story of a dance marathon, and the twisted series of events that leads Gloria, the main female character, to become utterly despondent and on the verge of committing suicide. She pulls out a gun in order to kill herself, but she is unable to pull the trigger. She turns to Robert and pleads for his help. Robert acquiesces to her request and shoots her in the head. When questioned by the police as to the motive for his action, Robert responds: "They shoot horses, don't they?"

As bizarre as this plot may seem, the logic behind Robert's decision to kill Gloria is materially no different from the logic behind those who support assisted suicide or euthanasia. If the killing of a suffering animal is an act of mercy, some say, then even more merciful is ending the life of a suffering person.

Before going any further, it is helpful to define a few terms. Euthanasia literally translated from the Greek means "good death", which is ironic considering euthanasia is the antithesis of dying well. While in ancient times, there was a general prohibition against it, Aristotle approved of euthanasia for deformed newborns in Sparta, and Plato declared that human beings with incurable illnesses should be left to die and that those who are mentally depraved should be put to death.[1]

In modern terms, euthanasia "is used to mean 'mercy killing,' for the purpose of putting an end to extreme suffering, or [s]aving abnormal babies, the mentally ill or the incurably sick from the prolongation, perhaps for many years of a miserable life, which could impose too heavy a burden on their families or on society."[2] Notice the emotionally charged words "extreme suffering", "miserable", and "burden".

---

[1] Elio Sgreccia, *Personalist Bioethics: Foundations and Applications*, trans. John Di Camillo and Michael Miller (Broomall, Penn.: National Catholic Bioethics Center, 2012), 664.

[2] Sacred Congregation for the Doctrine of the Faith, *Declaration on Euthanasia*, May 5, 1980.

Technically speaking, assisted suicide occurs when one person helps another person commit suicide but does not perform the action that leads to the other's death. Typically, a physician prescribes medications to the person wishing to die but does not administer those medications. Euthanasia is performed when someone actively participates in the death of the other: a physician or nurse infuses lethal medications into the veins of the person wishing to die. The intention of the parties involved is at the heart of the matter: "By euthanasia is understood an action or an omission which of itself or by intention causes death, in order that all suffering may in this way be eliminated."[3] There really is no ethical distinction between assisted suicide and euthanasia because both intend the death of someone, so for practical purposes, the terms are interchangeable. A more detailed look at the moral issues will follow.

Historical Context

Euthanasia and assisted suicide burst into the American public square in 1990, when Dr. Jack Kevorkian, a retired Michigan pathologist, agreed to meet Janet Adkins in his Volkswagen van, where he had placed his "suicide machine" consisting of three chemical solutions fed into an intravenous line. Kevorkian tried five times to insert the needle before eventually succeeding. Adkins then pressed a lever that released the drugs into her body, resulting in her death.[4]

[3] Sacred Congregation for the Doctrine of the Faith, *Declaration on Euthanasia*.

[4] Pamela Warrick, "Suicide's Partner: Is Jack Kevorkian an angel of mercy, or is he a killer, as some critics charge? 'Society is making me Dr. Death,' he says. 'Why can't they see? I'm Dr. Life!'", *Los Angeles Times*, December 6, 1992, latimes.com/archives/la-xpm-1992-12-06-vw-3171-story.html.

Before being sent to prison, Kevorkian claimed to have assisted in more than 130 suicides. In 1999, he was convicted of second-degree murder and the unlawful delivery of a controlled substance and sentenced to ten to twenty-five years in prison. In 2007, after having served fewer than nine years of his sentence, he was released on parole for good behavior.[5]

While Kevorkian's crimes threw a spotlight on the subject, the push for assisted suicide and euthanasia has its roots in the so-called "social Darwinism" that arose in the late 1800s following the publication of Darwin's *On the Origin of Species*. In a nutshell, social Darwinists held that superior genetic traits enabled certain societies to prevail over those with inferior genetic traits. To ward off degradation of the genetic pool, social Darwinists encouraged sterilizing and even killing individuals perceived as genetically inferior. Darwin's cousin Francis Galton coined the term "eugenics" for the measures a society would have to take to correct the disparity between productive members of society and those viewed as defective. The eugenics movement was tragically effective, with forty-one U.S. states enacting legislation mandating forced sterilization of the mentally disabled. These laws were supported by the U.S. Supreme Court decision in *Buck v. Bell*, which upheld a Virginia law that allowed for the involuntary sterilization of inmates in state institutions who were deemed to be suffering from hereditary insanity or imbecility.[6]

The same rationale that led to forced sterilizations was used to support euthanasia. In 1937, a bill was introduced

---

[5] *Encyclopedia Britannica*, s.v. Jack Kevorkian, by Ellen Bernstein, updated February 15, 2023, britannica.com/biography/Jack-Kevorkian.

[6] Neil Gorsuch, *The Future of Assisted Suicide and Euthanasia* (Princeton, N.J.: Princeton University Press, 2006), 34.

to the Nebraska legislature that allowed not only for the voluntary euthanasia of adults of sound mind suffering from a fatal illness, but also for the involuntary killing of the mentally incompetent or fatally ill.[7] While the state legislature never took up the bill, it set the stage for the establishment of the Euthanasia Society of America (ESA). One of the leaders of the ESA, Charles Potter, was quoted by the *New York Times*:

> Incurable imbeciles and persons suffering severe pain should have their misery ended by merciful methods. . . . I am in favor of euthanasia for sane people under certain definite conditions. They must suffer severe pain and . . . the disease is incurable. . . . When they [imbeciles] are hopelessly incurable, I would recommend that they be killed as mercifully as possible. I think it would be vastly more moral to kill off the incurable imbeciles and use the money for the children of the State.[8]

Support for the American euthanasia movement diminished following World War II as stories of Nazi euthanasia practices became known. In addition to the murder of millions of Jews and Christians, the Nazis killed approximately two hundred thousand disabled and elderly persons and forcibly sterilized four hundred thousand state wards.[9] Wary Americans recognized an equivalence between the eugenic policies of the Third Reich and the goals of the ESA.

As the memory of the atrocities of World War II faded, interest in euthanasia grew. In 1984, the Netherlands Supreme Court voted to allow euthanasia under certain circumstances,

[7] Legislative Bill 135, Nebraska Legislature, 52nd session (1937), as cited by Gorsuch, *Future of Assisted Suicide*, 35.

[8] "Dr. Potter Backs 'Mercy Killings'", *New York Times*, February 3, 1936.

[9] Gorsuch, *Future of Assisted Suicide*, 36–37.

and since 2001, physician-assisted suicide was effectively
legalized. Belgium soon followed suit, and as of now, under certain circumstances, physician-assisted suicide is legal
in Australia, Austria, Belgium, Canada, Colombia, Luxem-
bourg, the Netherlands, Spain, New Zealand, Switzerland,
and parts of the United States (California, Colorado, Hawaii,
Maine, New Jersey, New Mexico, Oregon, Vermont, Washington, and Washington, D.C.).[10]

To get a sense of the current scope of the problem, it is
helpful to look at statistics from Oregon, the first state to
legalize physician-assisted suicide in the United States. Oregon's Death with Dignity Act (DWDA) "allows terminally
ill individuals to end their lives through the voluntary self-
administration of lethal medications, expressly prescribed by
a physician for that purpose".[11] Since the law was passed in
1997, a total of 2,895 people have received prescriptions
under the DWDA, and 1,905 people (66%) have died from
ingesting the medications.

The DWDA outlines specific patient requirements to participate. A patient must be (1) eighteen years of age or older,
(2) a resident of Oregon, (3) capable of making and communicating health-care decisions to health-care practitioners, and (4) diagnosed with a terminal illness that will lead
to death within six months. The attending and consulting
physicians must determine whether a patient meets these
requirements and report that fact to the Oregon Health Authority at the time a prescription is written. Patients must

[10] Avivah Wittenberg-Cox, "A Designed Death—Where & When the
World Allows It", *Forbes*, October 22, 2022, forbes.com/sites/avivahwittenbe
rgcox/2022/10/22/a-designed-death--where--when-the-world-allows-it/?sh=
67b7e6de7b3d.

[11] Oregon Health Authority, "Death with Dignity Act", accessed May 23,
2022, https://www.oregon.gov/oha/ph/providerpartnerresources/evaluation
research/deathwithdignityact.

make two verbal requests to their doctor for the medication at least fifteen days apart.

According to the 2021 data summary, 383 people were reported to have received prescriptions under the DWDA. As of January 21, 2022, 238 people had died from ingesting the prescribed medications, including 20 who had received prescriptions in previous years. Demographic characteristics of DWDA patients were similar to those of previous years: most patients were aged sixty-five years or older (81%) and white (95%). The most common diagnosis was cancer (61%), followed by neurological disease (15%) and heart disease (12%). Notably only two of these patients were referred for psychiatric evaluation prior to the dispensing of the prescriptions.[12]

The three most frequently reported end-of-life concerns were loss of autonomy (93%), decreasing ability to participate in activities that made life enjoyable (92%), and loss of dignity (68%). Uncontrolled pain or concern about it was present in only 27%. A total of 133 physicians wrote 383 prescriptions during 2021 (1–47 prescriptions per physician). Time from ingestion until death ranged from two minutes to twenty-four hours, with a median time of thirty-two minutes.

Until recently, a patient had to be a resident of Oregon to receive prescriptions for lethal medications. Washington, California, Colorado, Hawaii, Maine, New Jersey, New Mexico, Vermont, and Washington, D.C. all include similar residency requirements. On March 21, 2022, the Oregon Health Authority, the Oregon Medical Board, and

---

[12] Public Health Division, Center for Health Statistics, "Oregon Death with Dignity Act: 2021 Data Summary", February 28, 2022, https://www.oregon.gov/oha/PH/PROVIDERPARTNERRESOURCES/EVALUATIONRESEARCH/DEATHWITHDIGNITYACT/Documents/year24.pdf.

the Multnomah County District Attorney's Office agreed that they "would not apply or otherwise enforce" the residency requirement.[13] The settlement still calls for the Oregon medical authorities to ask the state legislature to strike the residency language from the law but this is widely expected to occur. Advocates said they would use the settlement to press the eight other states and Washington, D.C., with medically assisted suicide laws to drop their residency requirements as well. Patients can now travel to Oregon to receive fatal doses of medications, making the state an assisted suicide destination, similar to Switzerland, where in a five-year period 611 people came from thirty-one countries, mostly from Germany and Britain: 44 percent and 21 percent of the total, respectively. Twenty-one people came from the United States.[14]

Cultural Context

How did we get to this point? How is it that multiple countries have legalized the killing of a person who requests to be killed because of unbearable suffering? By its nature, suffering is an internal struggle. No two people experience pain in the same fashion. The degree of physical or emotional pain does not necessarily correlate with the degree of suffering. For this reason, the criterion of "unbearable" suffering becomes entirely arbitrary. Modern society has developed a utilitarian perspective, where life is judged worthy only

[13] Raja Razek, "Oregon Will Stop Enforcing Residency Requirement in State's Death with Dignity Act", March 29, 2022, cnn.com/2022/03/29/us/oregon-stop-residency-requirement-death-with-dignity-act/index.html.

[14] Saskia Gauthier, Julian Mausbach, Thomas Reich, and Christine Bartsch, "Suicide Tourism: A Pilot Study on the Swiss Phenomenon", *Journal of Medical Ethics* 41, no. 8 (August 2015):612.

to the extent of its quality as measured by the presence or absence of certain physical or psychological function. Compassion has been twisted into the conclusion that it is better to die than to suffer.

In *Evangelium vitae*, John Paul II looked closely at the cultural movements that have led to an acceptance of euthanasia. First, he identified a cultural climate that considers suffering to be an evil to be avoided at all costs. In addition, he noted "there exists in contemporary culture a certain Promethean attitude which leads people to think that they can control life and death by taking the decisions about them into their own hands."[15] (In Greek mythology, Prometheus defied the gods by stealing fire and giving it to men.) This is the core value of the organizations that promote laws legalizing euthanasia and strive to "ensure people with terminal illness can decide for themselves what a good death means in accordance with their values and beliefs."[16] Furthermore, John Paul observed that choices that in themselves are evil have been held up as

> legitimate expressions of individual freedom, to be acknowledged and protected as actual rights. . . . Precisely in an age when the inviolable rights of the person are solemnly proclaimed and the value of life is publicly affirmed, the very right to life is being denied or trampled upon, especially at the more significant moments of existence: the moment of birth and the moment of death.[17]

At the root of this problem is the notion of an absolute freedom that elevates the isolated individual, creating a clash

[15] John Paul II, encyclical letter *Evangelium vitae* (The Gospel of Life) (March 25, 1995), no. 15.

[16] "About Us", Death with Dignity, accessed March 14, 2023, deathwith dignity.org/about/.

[17] John Paul II, *Evangelium vitae*, no. 16.

between the freedom of the strong and the freedom of the weak. Understood in this way,

> freedom negates and destroys itself and becomes a factor leading to the destruction of others. . . . If promotion of the self is understood in terms of absolute autonomy, people inevitably reach the point of rejecting one another. . . . To claim the right to abortion, infanticide and euthanasia, and to recognize that right in law, means to attribute to human freedom a perverse and evil significance: that of an absolute power over others and against others. This is the death of true freedom.[18]

The Congregation for the Doctrine of the Faith under Pope Francis has also identified growing individualism as a cultural obstacle that obscures the sacred value of life: the other is viewed as a limitation or threat to one's freedom. "Those who find themselves in a state of dependence and unable to realize a perfect autonomy or reciprocity, come to be cared for as a *favor* to them."[19] The letter notes that Pope Francis has spoken of a " 'throw-away culture' where victims are the weakest human beings, 'discarded' when the system aims for efficiency at all costs."[20] Human life is increasingly valued on the basis of efficiency and utility to the point where those who do not fit this criterion are unworthy lives.

In addition to modern culture's misguided conception of freedom, the rise of secularism is also at the root of the acceptance of euthanasia. The heart of this tragedy is the loss of the sense of God, which inevitably leads to the loss

[18] John Paul II, *Evangelium vitae*, nos. 19–20.

[19] Congregation for the Doctrine of the Faith, Letter on the Care of Persons in the Critical and Terminal Phases of Life *Samaritanus bonus* (The Good Samaritan) (July 14, 2020).

[20] Congregation for the Doctrine of the Faith, *Samaritanus bonus*.

of the sense of man: "Man is no longer able to see himself as 'mysteriously different' from other earthly creatures; he regards himself as merely one more living being, as an organism which, at most, has reached a very high stage of perfection."[21] They shoot horses, don't they?

The Reality of Euthanasia and Assisted Suicide

As mentioned, "euthanasia" is literally translated "good death", and those who favor its legalization often misrepresent the macabre reality of its practice. The argument is similar to the pro-abortion stance: we certainly do not want to go back to the days of back-alley abortions, so let's keep abortion safe and legal. Likewise, we certainly do not want to go back to the days of people being euthanized in the back of a van (*á la* Jack Kevorkian), so let's legalize assisted suicide, keeping it safe and "clean". Ironically, the criticism against modern medicine (it's too rigid, cold, and sterile) is being used as an argument for assisted suicide (let's make the process of dying tidy and convenient).

The 2016 movie *Me before You* was promoted as a romantic drama, depicting the sacrificial love that Louisa has for Will, a handsome, previously athletic man who was paralyzed in an accident. Will is understandably despondent, and Louisa does everything she can to prove to him that life is still worth living. Despite her efforts, Will follows through with his plans to travel to Switzerland and experience a peaceful death. Initially reluctant to accompany Will, at the last moment Louisa joins him at an idyllic, peaceful spa of sorts, where he draws his final breath in her arms. That's the Hollywood version of assisted suicide. That's the

---

[21] John Paul II, *Evangelium vitae*, no. 22.

myth its supporters want you to believe. But if you look at the published medical literature, the reality is something altogether different.

Myth: Physician-assisted suicide is universally successful, painless, and peaceful.

Truth: In a *New England Journal of Medicine* study from the Netherlands, a significant number of patients attempting physician-assisted suicide experienced complications, including vomiting, inability to finish the medication, a longer-than-expected time before death, failure to induce coma, and awakening from coma. In many of these patients, the attending physician then administered a lethal medication to complete the job.[22]

Myth: Patients who die by physician-assisted suicide are properly screened to rule out and treat psychiatric illnesses.

Truth: In a study published in the *British Medical Journal*, one in four Oregon patients requesting physician aid in dying had clinical depression. Of those who ultimately died by lethal ingestion, one in three met criteria for depression and should have been excluded by the Oregon Death with Dignity Act.[23]

Myth: Adequate oversight exists to prevent assisted suicide abuses.

Truth: A letter published in the *Journal of the American Medical Association* documents doctor shopping to circumvent safeguards against economic pressures and coercion, lethal

[22] Johanna H. Groenewoud et al., "Clinical Problems with the Performance of Euthanasia and Physician-Assisted Suicide in the Netherlands", *New England Journal of Medicine* 342 (February, 2000): 551–56.

[23] Linda Ganzini, Elizabeth R. Goy, and Steven K. Dobscha, "Prevalence of Depression and Anxiety in Patients Requesting Physicians' Aid in Dying: Cross Sectional Survey", *British Medical Journal* 337 (October 8, 2008), bmj.com/content/337/bmj.a1682.

medications being administered by someone other than the requesting patient, and lethal medications being given without a doctor's prescription.[24]

Myth: Physician-assisted suicide is available only for terminally ill patients.

Truth: The slippery slope of assisted suicide is demonstrated in the Netherlands, where physician-assisted suicide and euthanasia for unbearable suffering were legalized in 2002. Over time, the definition of unbearable suffering has been broadened, leading to the use of assisted suicide or euthanasia in a growing number of patients without a terminal disease. In a study published in the *Journal of the American Medical Association*, more than 25 percent of patients who were "tired of living" were granted their request for physician-assisted suicide or euthanasia. Almost 50 percent of those whose requests were granted characterized part of their suffering as loneliness. More than 50 percent of granted requests were for people over eighty years old, raising additional red flags.[25]

The dark truth of physician-assisted suicide is far from the tranquil picture painted by death with dignity advocates. Whether it is a matter of botched suicide attempts or lack of compliance with established safeguards, history has shown that physician-assisted suicide is problematic at multiple levels.

[24] Kenneth Stevens and William Toffler, "Euthanasia and Physician-Assisted Suicide", *Journal of the American Medical Association* 316, no. 15 (October 18, 2016), 1599.

[25] Scott Y. H. Kim, Raymond G. De Vries, and John R. Peteet, "Euthanasia and Assisted Suicide of Patients with Psychiatric disorders in the Netherlands 2011 to 2014", *Journal of the American Medical Association Psychiatry* 73, no. 4 (April 2016): 362–68.

Moral Concerns

Euthanasia and assisted suicide are acts or omissions that intend to cause death and eliminate suffering. The intent of the patient and the intent of the medical provider are at the heart of the issue. Assisted suicide and euthanasia must be distinguished from the legitimate decision to withdraw or withhold medical care that is no longer beneficial and is excessively burdensome. For example, the decision to stop chemotherapy treatments for a cancer patient who is nearing death can be an appropriate decision. The intent of such a decision is not to bring about or hasten death, but rather to accept the human condition in the face of death.

From a moral perspective, the Church has consistently taught that "euthanasia is a grave violation of the law of God, since it is the deliberate and morally unacceptable killing of a human person. This doctrine is based upon the natural law and upon the written word of God."[26] While certain psychological or social situations may reduce or even eliminate the responsibility of someone who commits suicide, the action of suicide remains objectively immoral, and to cooperate with another person's intent to commit suicide can never be excused. Centuries ago, Saint Augustine wrote, "It is never licit to kill another: even if he should wish it, indeed if he request it."[27] Even if a person asks for assistance in suicide, it is never morally permissible: "just as we cannot make another person our slave, even if they ask to be, so

[26] John Paul II, *Evangelium vitae*, no. 65.

[27] St. Augustine, "Letter 204", no. 3, in St. Augustine, *The Works of Saint Augustine: A Translation for the 21st Century*, Vol. II/3, *Letters 156–210*, trans. Roland Testke, S.J., ed. Boniface Ramsey (Hyde Park, N.Y.: New City Press, 2004), 372.

we cannot directly choose to take the life of another, even if they request it."[28]

As John Paul wrote, "Euthanasia must be called a false mercy, and indeed a disturbing 'perversion' of mercy. True 'compassion' leads to sharing another's pain; it does not kill the person whose suffering we cannot bear."[29] The perversity of euthanasia is made worse when carried out by family members, who are supposed to love the sick person, and physicians, who are supposed to care for the sick person.

Pope Francis wrote on the pastoral discernments that need to be made regarding those who request assisted suicide or euthanasia. Absolution cannot be given in advance, and such persons have decided upon a gravely immoral act and willingly persist in this decision. A penitent can receive the Sacraments of Penance, with absolution and anointing, and Viaticum only when the minister discerns his readiness to take concrete steps that indicate he has modified his decision. "To delay absolution is a medicinal act of the Church, intended not to condemn, but to lead the sinner to conversion."[30] However, it is necessary to stay close to the person unable to receive the sacraments as an invitation to conversion, and it remains possible to accompany the person whose decision may be changed. "Nevertheless, those who spiritually assist these persons should avoid any gesture, such as remaining until the euthanasia is performed, that could be interpreted as approval of this action."[31]

In the United States, supporters of assisted suicide attempt to distinguish between it and euthanasia. Assisted suicide is

[28] Congregation for the Doctrine of the Faith, *Samaritanus bonus*.

[29] John Paul II, *Evangelium vitae*, no. 66.

[30] Congregation for the Doctrine of the Faith, *Samaritanus bonus*.

[31] Congregation for the Doctrine of the Faith, *Samaritanus bonus*.

intentionally *helping* another person to kill himself, while euthanasia is *intentionally killing* the person (with his permission). Their claim is that with assisted suicide, the physician who prescribes the drugs is a passive participant, while the physician who injects medications into the veins of the patient is an active participant.[32] This is a false distinction; in either scenario, the physician's actions are necessary for the patient to die. An internist is responsible for the complications associated with a medication just as a surgeon is responsible for the complications associated with a surgery.

The gravity of euthanasia is made even worse when it is performed on someone who has not requested or consented to it. Infants and children are clearly unable to give consent to any medical treatment. Yet, in the Netherlands, it is legal to give medications intended to hasten death to pediatric patients.[33,34] Modern-day "right to die" ideology is rooted in the eugenics movement of the early twentieth century. Certain lives were considered not worth living, and as mentioned above, the founder of the Euthanasia Society of America believed that "incurable imbeciles and persons suffering severe pain should have their misery ended by merciful methods."[35] This horrific recommendation is nothing short of premeditated murder.

[32] Nicholas Dixon, "On the Difference between Physician-Assisted Suicide and Active Euthanasia", *Hastings Center Report* 28, no. 5 (September–October 1998): 25–29.

[33] A. van der Heide et al,. "Medical End-of-Life Decisions Made for Neonates and Infants in the Netherlands", *Lancet* 350, no. 9073 (July 26, 1997):251–55.

[34] Astrid M. Vrakking et al., "Medical End-of-Life Decisions for Children in the Netherlands", *The Archives of Pediatrics & Adolescent Medicine* 159, no. 9 (2005): 802–9.

[35] "Dr. Potter Backs 'Mercy Killings'", *New York Times*, February 3, 1936.

Legal Arguments against Assisted Suicide

Supreme Court Justice Neil Gorsuch has written extensively about the legal arguments for and against assisted suicide and euthanasia. To date, the Supreme Court has not yet weighed in on its legality, but has allowed states to establish their own laws. As mentioned previously, assisted suicide is currently legal in California, Colorado, Hawaii, Maine, New Jersey, New Mexico, Oregon, Vermont, Washington, and Washington, D.C. However, using secular moral theory, Gorsuch argues that human life is fundamentally and inherently valuable, and that the intentional taking of human life by private persons is always wrong.[36] He proposes that human life is a basic good, meaning that "its value is not instrumental, not dependent on any other condition or reason, but something intrinsically good in and of itself."[37] The Fourteenth Amendment to the U.S. Constitution guarantees equal protection under the law to all persons, and this protection is grounded in the belief that all persons have innate dignity and are worthy of respect regardless of their perceived value to society. As stated in the Declaration of Independence, "We hold these truths to be self-evident, that all men are created equal, that they are endowed by their Creator with certain unalienable Rights, that among these [is] Life." If human life is a basic good, it follows that we should refrain from actions intended to do it harm. Gorsuch makes the clear distinction between discontinuing care when death is foreseen and seeking to bring about the death of a person:

[36] Neil Gorsuch, *The Future of Assisted Suicide and Euthanasia* (Princeton, N.J.: Princeton University Press, 2006), 157.
[37] Gorsuch, *Future of Assisted Suicide*, 158.

Patients may choose to reject care and accept death only to be left unmolested by further invasive treatment, to be left in peace to die, to avoid imposing further burdens on loved ones, or just to leave the hospital and go home. Such choices and others like them are made not out of any suicidal impulse but out of a recognition of the inevitability of death, an acceptance of it, and an intention only to avoid further burdens, be left in peace, return to family, and so forth.[38]

Laws that permit assisted suicide treat the lives of different persons quite differently, thus violating the Equal Protection Clause of the Fourteenth Amendment. For the healthy, life is legally inviolable, and no person can take it. For the terminally ill, life is violable and those who help take it are exempt from criminal liability. Laws such as Oregon's argue that assisted suicide is allowed to preserve the autonomy of dying patients, yet that same autonomy is not allowed in any other group of patients. Autonomy is preserved for some patients, but not others. Again, the Equal Protection Clause is violated.[39]

Freedom and Compassion

As we have seen, respect for autonomy and compassion toward the suffering patient are the two main principles used to justify euthanasia. Self-determination—the ability to decide for oneself—is highly valued in Western cultures. However, while autonomy and self-determination are goods deserving respect, they are not absolute goods. Life is a fundamental good deserving of respect in all situations, even if the patient feels otherwise.

[38] Gorsuch, *Future of Assisted Suicide*, 165.
[39] Gorsuch, *Future of Assisted Suicide*, 178–79.

The appeal to compassion brings us full circle to our starting point: "They shoot horses, don't they?" Advocates for assisted suicide argue that no one should endure pointless suffering, and one of the roles of medicine is to relieve suffering. Therefore, physicians should make assisted suicide available to terminally ill patients as a merciful way to relieve them of their pain. However, as John Paul stated,

> *Euthanasia* is one of those tragedies caused by an ethic that claims to dictate who should live and who should die. Even if it is motivated by sentiments of a misconstrued compassion or of a misunderstood preservation of dignity, euthanasia actually eliminates the person instead of relieving the individual of suffering. . . .
>
> True compassion, on the contrary, encourages every reasonable effort for the patient's recovery. At the same time, it helps draw the line when it is clear that no further treatment will serve this purpose.[40]

Dying patients should be lovingly accompanied to the end of their lives by people helping them "to prepare their souls for the encounter with the Heavenly Father". "Even when medical treatment is unable to defeat a serious pathology, all its possibilities are directed to the alleviation of suffering." Palliative care (covered in greater detail elsewhere) can successfully address all types of suffering—physical, emotional, and spiritual. This is true compassion.

---

[40] John Paul II, Address to the Participants of the 19th International Conference of the Pontifical Council for Pastoral Health Care (November 12, 2004), nos. 3–4.

8

COVID and Dying Alone

As a freshly minted nursing school graduate, Samantha was eager to plunge headfirst into the cauldron of care known as the ICU. Every nascent skill learned during clinical rotations was quickly honed by treating critically ill patients with the latest technology. The term *cura personalis* denotes care for all aspects of a person's health, from the physical to the mental and the spiritual, and as an ICU nurse, Samantha embodied this approach, even though she probably had never heard the term *cura personalis*. During her first year as a nurse, she accompanied patients and their families through the "normal" process of dying. By normal, I mean dying patients and families were allowed to be together to the extent they desired, and support from friends and clergy was also available. Dying was never easy, but Samantha felt prepared and the hope of heaven buoyed her heart.

COVID changed everything. The sheer volume of sick patients teetering on the brink of death overwhelmed hospitals. COVID ICU floors were jerry-rigged from units typically used for colonoscopies or other minor procedures. Pre-COVID, Samantha might have covered two or at the most three patients at a time; at the height of the various waves, that number ballooned to five or even six patients. Critical care nursing devolved into medical whack-a-mole, rushing from one near catastrophe to the next, all the while weighed down by double gowns, double masks, double gloves. Communication with families was bare-boned, a brief phone call squeezed in before "proning" the next ventilated patient.[1] It was physically exhausting, emotionally draining, and spiritually numbing.

The elderly were particularly hard hit by the pandemic. In 2022, people sixty-five years and older represent approximately 16 percent of the U.S. population[2] yet 75 percent of COVID-related deaths occurred in this age group.[3] Especially during the early stages of the pandemic, COVID patients eighty years or older on ventilators had fatality rates higher than 90 percent. According to the Hastings Center, "For the vast majority of older patients with respiratory failure, ventilators did not provide life-saving treatment. . . . Despite the use of ventilators, we neither saved lives nor provided a good death for these patients."[4]

COVID restrictions kept patients and families apart, and the isolation felt by patients was exacerbated by the layers of personal protection equipment (PPE) that made nurses look like they were from outer space. Hugs were never a consideration. At best, a nitrile-covered hand provided a modicum of human touch. There was just not enough time to do much more.

So many people died that it is difficult for Samantha to

---

[1] In order to optimize lung function, critically ill COVID patients were placed in the prone position, a process that was made exceptionally difficult by the need for mechanical ventilation and a multitude of monitoring devices attached to or inserted in the patient.

[2] "Older Americans Month: May 2022" (press release), United States Census Bureau, May 2022, accessed March 14, 2022, census.gov/newsroom/stories/older-americans-month.html.

[3] "COVID-19 Mortality Overview", Centers for Disease Control and Prevention, accessed September 20, 2022, cdc.gov/nchs/covid19/mortality-overview.htm.

[4] Tia Powell, Eran Bellin, and Amy R. Ehrlich, "Older Adults and Covid-19: The Most Vulnerable, the Hardest Hit", *Hastings Center Report* 50, no. 3 (June 29, 2020), DOI: 10.1002/hast.1136.

remember the details of any given case. Just as soon as one person died, the room was quickly cleaned, and another critically ill patient filled the spot. Samantha did her very best to bring comfort, but truth be told, by the time a COVID patient was near death, he was unconscious on a ventilator, unresponsive to whatever comfort she could offer. Plus, there was only so much comfort she could bring over the phone or by an iPad to the family who were forbidden to be at bedside. Pre-COVID, Samantha was the heart of the body of professionals caring for the dying; patients and families were deeply appreciative. With COVID, she became the target of anger and frustration, as she had no choice but to enforce the restrictive policies meant to tamp the spread of the virus and keep everyone as safe as possible.

It was a scene tragically played out countless times during the early waves of the COVID pandemic. The virus spread quickly. Natural immunity was absent. PPE was scarce. Vaccines were months away. Effective antiviral treatments had yet to be developed. Vulnerable people quickly succumbed to the virus. Hospitals, like everywhere else, were in lockdown. No visitors, especially for COVID patients. Even with death rapidly approaching, only medical personnel were allowed in a hospital room, while a single family member was allowed to watch through the window. Some hospital policies were even more restrictive, and families were barred from even entering the hospital. The final moments of life were witnessed by a cell phone video. No handholding. No kiss goodbye. No final embrace. No anointing. No Viaticum. No final confession. Death at a distance, confirmed as the monitor on the wall flatlined.

People with COVID were pariahs, twentieth-century lepers, isolated in basement bedrooms until the prescribed period of contagiousness passed. Outside, streets were empty. Stores were shuttered. Only "essential" industries continued to produce. Parks were closed. No lingering on a bench. No climbing jungle gyms.

The numbers are mind-numbing. As of March 2023, the Centers for Disease Control estimated over 1,100,000 Americans had died of COVID,[5] while the World Health Organization reported almost 6,900,000 deaths worldwide.[6] Many believe the numbers are actually substantially higher, as deaths were underreported in many poorer countries.

The fear of dying alone is nearly universal. Under normal circumstances, hospitals go to great lengths to bring families together with a loved one who is approaching death. Not so with COVID, and this led to great suffering for patients, families, and caregivers. Especially during the first year of the pandemic, hospitals were closed to visitors, regardless of the patient's diagnosis. COVID and non-COVID patients alike were isolated from family and friends. Noncritical patients could communicate by cell phone, but ICU patients who were sedated on a ventilator were effectively stranded on a medical desert island with no means of communication. Moral distress was experienced by families and health-care workers. Families expressed feeling helpless, deeply troubled, and guilty that they could not provide comfort and support at a time when it was most needed. Health-care providers were the recipients of families' sorrows and complaints, leaving them with a sense of frustration and helplessness.[7] It was a lose-lose scenario.

[5] "COVID-19 Mortality", Centers for Disease Control and Prevention, accessed March 14, 2023, cdc.gov/nchs/covid19/mortality-overview.htm.

[6] "WHO Coronavirus (COVID-19) Dashboard", World Health Organization, accessed March 14, 2023, covid19.who.int/.

[7] Sujin Ann-Yi, Ahsan Azhar, and Eduardo Bruera, "Dying Alone during a Pandemic", *Journal of Palliative Medicine* 24, no. 12 (November 17, 2021): 1905–8.

Samantha tells the story of one case that epitomizes her experience as a COVID ICU nurse. John was fifty-one years old with two daughters. He was generally healthy and was not considered at high risk for dying from COVID. Despite the most effective treatments of the time, he continued to deteriorate and was transferred to the ICU, where he spent the last three weeks of his life. At least initially, John was well enough to communicate with his nurses and with his family via iPad. But when he declined further, he was intubated and placed on a ventilator. The combination of sedating medicines and hypoxia made him unresponsive to any verbal communication. Even though the family had a sense of how bad he was doing, the gravity of the situation did not translate well over the jerky images on Facetime, and his family understandably continued to want everything done to keep him alive. John coded on three consecutive days: his blood pressure dropped to imperceptible and his heart contracted ineffectively, necessitating prolonged periods of chest compressions, multiple electrical shocks to the heart, and syringe upon syringe of adrenaline-like medications to shore up his blood flow.

Through all this, the family was barred from the hospital. When John coded for the third time, his family did not want him to die in their absence, so again everything possible was done. Hospital staff performed chest compressions off and on for over three hours to the point of physical exhaustion, necessitating the use of a mechanical external chest compressor when they no longer had the strength. Realizing the futility of further care, yet wanting to be with John at his final moments, John's family drove to the hospital, ignored the rules, and burst into the room as he was being coded. Witnessing the reality of the situation, the family called off the code and sat by John's side during his final moments, while Samantha and the other exhausted staff stood by, ready to prepare the room for the next patient.

Ars Moriendi

In 1346–1353, the black plague engulfed Europe and killed more than a quarter of the population. About twenty-five million Europeans died from the plague. The disease was endemic well into the fifteenth century, continuing to claim countless lives. The COVID-19 pandemic invites comparison to the black plague. COVID-19 and the black plague have significant differences: COVID is caused by a respiratory virus, while the black plague was spread by rat fleas carrying the bacterium *Yersinia pestis*.[8] When this bacteria traveled through the bloodstream of an infected person to his lungs, it caused a secondary infection called pneumonic plague. And this disease, like COVID, was spread from one person to another through respiratory droplets released by coughing or sneezing.[9] The two pandemics have other similarities: both originated in China and spread by international travel; economies slumped in their aftermath; and death was indiscriminate, killing rich and poor alike. And much like the COVID pandemic, dying patients during the plague were separated from family and clergy. People died alone.

In the fifteenth century, a text of unknown authorship circulated in Europe. *Ars Moriendi*, the Art of Dying, was written as a guide for dying persons who had limited ac-

---

[8] *Encyclopedia Britannica*, s.v. "Black Death", updated January 2, 2023, britannica.com/event/Black-Death/Cause-and-outbreak.

[9] "Frequently Asked Questions about Plague", Centers for Disease Control and Prevention, https://emergency.cdc.gov/agent/plague/faq.asp#: :text= If%20bubonic%20plague%20is%20not,secondary%20case%20of%20pneum onic%20plague.

cess to priests and the sacraments, which was widely the case during the black plague. It was intended to be read in advance of impending death as a way to prepare for death while a person still had the wherewithal to read and reflect. The shorter version of the text focused on the temptations faced by the dying and the remedies for them and included woodblock illustrations to help those who could not read. The more things change, the more they stay the same, and the temptations during the black plague described in *Ars Moriendi* were also seen during the COVID pandemic. *Even if the threat of death is not imminent, the fear of death can bring about the same temptations faced by a person who is actually dying.* These behaviors can be seen at both the individual and societal levels.

Ars Moriendi begins with the assertion that the death of the soul is to be feared much more than the death of the body. "The devil knows how precious the soul is, and so he assails the dying person with the greatest temptations in order to secure his eternal death. Hence, it is of the utmost importance for the dying person to tend carefully to his soul, so it will not perish at the time of death."[10]

The first temptation faced by the dying person is the temptation of the devil concerning faith: "Faith is the foundation of all salvation, and without it no one can be saved. . . . And so the devil, the enemy of the entire human race, attempts with all his strength to turn the dying person entirely away from faith."[11]

When the initial wave of COVID-19 washed over the world, countries went into lockdown: only essential services were allowed to operate. With schools closed, most

[10] *The Art of Dying: A New Annotated Translation*, trans. Br. Columba Thomas, O.P., M.D. (Philadelphia: National Catholic Bioethics Center, 2021), 37.

[11] *Art of Dying*, 43.

students, from kindergarten to graduate school, were forced into remote learning, with teachers presenting classwork via internet-based video conferencing. Likewise, churches were closed and services accessed via the internet. Despite the separation between congregations and clergy, during the initial wave of the pandemic, many Americans reported that their faith was strengthened. According to a Pew Research Center survey, 24 percent of U.S. adults reported that their faith became stronger because of the pandemic, while 2 percent said their faith became weaker and 47 percent said their faith was unchanged.[12] Christians, particularly historically black Protestants, were especially likely to report that their faith increased during the pandemic.

So, at first it seemed that the temptation to lose faith was not much of a problem during the initial stages of the pandemic. This is probably not too surprising; traumatic events often bring out a sense of religiosity. No atheists in foxholes.

But as the pandemic continued to grind on, with second, third, even fourth waves, things began to change. The temptation to lose faith became more problematic. A German study reported that after the first wave and lockdown, faith in a "Higher Source" and loss of faith were stable for several months. However, during the second wave and lockdown, there was a continuous decrease in trust in a Higher Source and a constant increase in loss of faith. This was seen across all age groups and Christian denominations.[13]

---

[12] Claire Gecewicz, "Few Americans Say Their House of Worship Is Open, but a Quarter Say Their Faith Has Grown amid the Pandemic", Pew Research Center, April 30, 2020, pewresearch.org/fact-tank/2020/04/30/few-americans-say-their-house-of-worship-is-open-but-a-quarter-say-their-religious-faith-has-grown-amid-pandemic/.

[13] Arndt Büssing, Klaus Baumann, and Janusz Surzykiewicz, "Loss of Faith and Decrease in Trust in a Higher Source During COVID-19 in Germany", *Journal of Religion and Health* 61 (February 2022):741–66.

Again, this is probably not all that surprising. When faced with an acute emergency, many people lean into their faith, but as the situation transitions to a more chronic problem, fatigue settles in and can be accompanied by cynicism or indifference. The temptation to lose faith becomes more likely as things drag on.

According to *Ars Moriendi*, the next temptation is to despair: "The devil tempts the sick person to despair, which opposes the hope and confidence he should have in God. For when the sick person is tormented with bodily suffering, the devil compounds his suffering by assailing him with the memory of his sins, especially those he has not confessed, in order to make him despair."[14] Despair and loss of hope are synonymous, and loss of hope is a hallmark of depression and other forms of mental illness. Did the COVID pandemic create despair? Did the COVID pandemic worsen mental health outcomes?

Technically speaking, isolation is the separation of people who are infected from those who are not. Quarantine is the separation and restriction of movement of people who have potentially been exposed to an infectious agent. Often, the two terms are used interchangeably. Multiple studies revealed that longer durations of quarantine were associated with poorer mental health, specifically post-traumatic stress symptoms, avoidance behaviors, and anger. As would be expected, prolonged confinement brought boredom, frustration, and a sense of isolation. Having inadequate supplies (food, water, clothing) during quarantine was a source of frustration, anger, and anxiety that persisted for months. Inconsistent messaging from public health officials and lack of clarity about different levels of risk led to people fearing

[14] *Art of Dying*, 57.

the worst. Loss of income during quarantine was a significant risk factor for anger and anxiety that also persisted for
months. Especially in the early days of the pandemic, quar-
antined individuals experienced stigma after their period of
confinement, with others avoiding them, withdrawing social invitations, treating them with fear and suspicion, and
making critical comments.[15]

Sadness and fear are normal emotions that every person
experiences when faced with loss or danger. But prolonged
sadness and fear, which are sometimes medically diagnosed
as depression and anxiety disorders, can undermine a person's ability to fulfill his daily activities. They can also make
him more vulnerable to temptations.

Depression and anxiety disorders were the leading causes
of mental health burdens prior to the pandemic, and many
of the determinants of poor mental health were exacerbated
by the COVID-19 pandemic. Major depressive disorders
and anxiety disorders were significantly increased during
the pandemic, with females being more impacted than males
and younger age groups more affected than older age groups.
An additional 53 million cases of major depressive disorders
and 76 million anxiety disorders were due to the COVID-
19 pandemic, above and beyond the levels of anxiety and
depression documented prior to its onset.[16]

There is nothing new under the sun. The temptations of
the devil experienced during the black plague as described

[15] Samantha K. Brooks et al., "The Psychological Impact of Quarantine
and How to Reduce It: Rapid Review of the Evidence", *The Lancet* 395, no.
10227 (March 14, 2020): 912–20.

[16] COVID-19 Mental Disorders Collaborators, "Global Prevalence and
Burden of Depressive and Anxiety Disorders in 204 Countries and Territories
in 2020 Due to the COVID-19 Pandemic" (abstract), *Lancet* 398, no. 10312
(November 6, 2021):1700–12, National Library of Science, pubmed.ncbi.nlm
.nih.gov/34634250/.

hundreds of years ago in *Ars Moriendi* were the same temptations faced during the COVID pandemic. One such temptation is to avarice. One would think that as the threat of death looms, material possessions would no longer seem so important. Not so, according to *Ars Moriendi*:

> Avarice is the excessive preoccupation with the passing things of this world: wives and worldly friends, material wealth, and other things they have loved greatly in life. Through these things, the devil especially vexes a person at the point of death, saying "O wretch, soon you will leave behind all the temporal goods you have amassed with the greatest care and effort: even your wife, your children, your kindred, your dearest friends and all other desirable things of this world. Their companionship could be a great solace for you and an occasion of great good for them."[17]

During the COVID pandemic, as individuals faced the prospect of death, greed became a prominent motivator of behavior in studies that looked at purchase patterns. Fearing the unavailability of basic essentials, consumers developed a stockpiling mentality.[18] They hoarded things like massive amounts of toilet paper, more than could ever be used over many months.

The fear of illness and death may have driven some individuals to succumb to the temptation of greed, but this pales in comparison to the greed exhibited by corporations that benefited from the pandemic. While the pandemic has been devastating for rich countries like the United States and the United Kingdom, the world's poorest countries have been

[17] *Art of Dying*, 77.
[18] Kavya Satish, Abhishek Venkatesh, and Anand Shankar Raja Manivannan, "COVID-19 Is Driving Fear and Greed in Consumer Behavior and Purchase Pattern", *South Asian Journal of Marketing* 2, no. 2 (December 13, 2021), 113–19.

hardest hit, with women and children bearing a disproportionate burden. Lack of testing and reporting means that
very large numbers of deaths due to COVID-19 go unreported, especially in the poorest countries. For every death
in a high-income country, an estimated four other people
have died in a low- or lower-middle-income country. But not
everyone has been harmed by the pandemic, at least finan-
cially. A new billionaire is created every twenty-six hours,
and of the new billionaires created during the pandemic,
forty are COVID-19 billionaires, having profited from vaccines, treatments, tests, and PPE.[19]

The temptation to greed is closely related to the temptation to spiritual pride or "vainglory" as described in *Ars
Moriendi*: "The devil appeals to the sick person's vanity and
complacency, a form of spiritual pride. . . O how many
good things you have worked for! You should take tremendous pride in these things, since you are not like the others
who have committed endless sins . . . through pride man
presumes whatever good he has received from God comes
from himself." Pride and greed can lead to presumption
and a sense of entitlement. Pride leads to placing self before
others.

When the pandemic first arrived, major cities were the
first to be affected. Dense population enhanced transmission
of the virus, and impoverished people were less healthy to
begin with, making them particularly vulnerable. Recognizing this problem, many wealthy people fled to their summer
homes to avoid the densely packed cities, which were the
epicenters of the pandemic. During the black plague, the
wealthy did exactly the same, leaving cities in droves for

[19] Oxfam International, "Pandemic of Greed: A Wake-Up Call for Vaccine
Equity at a Grim Milestone", media briefing, March 3, 2022, 2, oxfam.org/en
/research/pandemic-greed.

their country estates. This strategy ultimately failed on multiple levels. Local residents clashed with seasonal residents, who were perceived as selfish tourists who put the permanent population at risk by bringing the virus with them and by depleting already-scarce resources. In the long run, the virus knew no geographic boundaries, and rural areas were equally impacted.

Whether death is imminent or a distant possibility, the same temptations can assail individuals and society as a whole. Whether it is the black plague in the Middle Ages or the COVID-19 pandemic, the fear of death can lead to temptations to loss of faith, despair, greed, and pride. But things are not hopeless, and each of these temptations can be overcome by the virtues of faith, hope, charity, and humility. However, these virtues must be cultivated throughout one's lifetime, for the preparation for death begins at birth. This is not meant to be done alone; we are to accompany each other in the preparation for death and during the time of death. As *Ars Moriendi* concludes:"Therefore, take note of the fact that in the end, the salvation of a person consists entirely in the preparation for death. Each one ought to attend carefully to this, providing for himself a devout, faithful and suitable relative or friend who will reliably assist him at the point of death—to constancy of faith, patience, devotion, trust and perseverance—by encouraging him, enlivening him and faithfully saying devotional prayers for him as he suffers."[20]

[20] *Art of Dying*, 86.

9

Deaths of Despair

Uncle Jack would give you the shirt off his back, but I was still afraid of him. He always seemed to have the countenance of a wounded bear. Jack and his three brothers prided themselves on being "pure Irish" even though they were two generations separated from the first Doran immigrants. The brooding Irishman is cliché, but that is my memory of Jack.

Though he lacked a college degree, he was able to support his family reasonably well as an electrician. The father of two sons and a daughter, Jack was married to Barb, who was afflicted with severe rheumatoid arthritis that progressively distorted her hands and feet. There was not just one reason why Jack became an alcoholic, and his lack of faith robbed him, perhaps, of sources for help in overcoming his addiction to alcohol. And I don't mean just the Catholic faith. The starting point for Alcoholics Anonymous is belief in a Higher Power.

Uncle Jack died a slow death over several years, punctuated by hospitalizations either directly related to his drinking or for other conditions associated with his alcoholism. Alcohol not only caused his health to deteriorate, as with so many other addicts, substance abuse also strained or even destroyed his relationships. A soured business venture with Jim, his younger brother, prompted Jack to sever any contact between the two, and Jack went to his grave without talking to his brother in over a decade.

Jack was only fifty-six years old when he died an igno-
minious death in the bathroom. Jack was a hulking man,
and it took an experienced "wagon guy" from the police
department and several men from the funeral home to ex-
tricate his body and carry it down the stairs. Jack had been
adamantly opposed to a funeral and wanted his body donated to science. Both directives were honored. The term
death of despair had not yet been coined at the time of his
death, but it perfectly fits Jack's end.

In 2014, Anne Case and Angus Deaton were in Varney
Bridge, Montana, enjoying their yearly mountain vacation.
They were trying to understand why this particular Montana county had a suicide rate four times higher than their
home county in New Jersey. As they continued with their
research, they discovered that suicide rates of middle-aged
white Americans were rising faster than in the rest of the
population. Moreover, while gleaning data from the Centers
for Disease Control, to their astonishment they found that
the rate of *total* deaths was also rising among middle-aged
white males.

With few exceptions, all-cause mortality had fallen year-
over-year throughout the twentieth century, with the exceptions of the influenza epidemic of 1918 and the excess mortality of young men during the AIDS/HIV epidemic of the
1990s. So, it was shocking to find that white, middle-aged
men were dying earlier than at any time in the past hundred years. Suicide alone could not explain the increase in
rising death rates, but when deaths from drug overdose and
alcoholic liver disease were included, the excess mortality
could be explained. White, middle-aged men were killing
themselves: sometimes abruptly through suicide, sometimes
more slowly through drug and alcohol addiction. They la-

beled the triad of death by suicide, drug overdose, or alcoholic liver disease "deaths of despair".[1]

Case and Deaton published their landmark findings in 2015, noting that if white mortality rates for ages forty-five to fifty-four had held at their 1998 value, 96,000 deaths would have been avoided from 1999 to 2013. If the mortality rates had continued to decline as they had previously from 1979 to 1998, *500,000 deaths could have been avoided in the period from 1999 to 2013.*[2] The CDC annually updates its statistics on causes of death, and in 2017, 185,000 people died from deaths of despair: suicide, drug overdose, and alcoholic cirrhosis.[3]

Addiction, suicide, and mental illness are closely linked. Those who suffer from depression are more likely to seek consolation from drugs or alcohol, which provide a temporary feeling of euphoria. When the momentary reprieve provided by the substance is gone, feelings of worthlessness deepen, leading someone further down the path of addiction. Addiction can be psychological or physical or both. In any case, when the euphoria wears off, a person addicted to a substance experiences shame, feelings of worthlessness, and depression, and death can seem to be a better alternative.

So, who are those dying a death of despair? Historically, suicides were more common among the educated, but in the current epidemic this is not the case. The majority of deaths

---

[1] Anne Case and Angus Deaton, *Deaths of Despair and the Future of Capitalism* (Princeton, N.J.: Princeton University Press, 2020).

[2] Anne Case and Angus Deaton, "Rising Morbidity and Mortality in Midlife among White Non-Hispanic Americans in the 21st Century", *The Proceedings of the National Academy of Sciences* 112, no. 49 (August 22, 2015): 15078–15083.

[3] Case and Deaton, *Deaths of Despair*, 94.

of despair in the Case/Deaton study occurred among those without a four-year college degree, in other words, members of the working class.[4]

There has been a widening gap of income and family stability between those with a bachelor's degree and those without. For white men without a four-year degree, median earnings adjusted for inflation fell 13 percent between 1979 and 2017, while national income per person grew 85 percent during the same period.[5] This decline in wages parallels a decline in job quality.[6] For those lacking a bachelor's degree, marriage rates have been declining and the proportion of children born out of wedlock has been increasing. While church membership in the United States as a whole has declined substantially in the past few decades, there is a significant and growing gap in weekly church attendance between those with a bachelor's degree and those without. Those with a bachelor's degree are significantly more likely to attend church than those without.[7] In other words, the white working class has been losing the support it once received from communities of faith. Staying away from church is another sign of feelings of shame, which is sadly ironic because Jesus came to heal the brokenhearted and to enrich those "poor in spirit".

It is important to note that African Americans historically and currently die younger, are less likely to go to college, and earn less than whites. However, since 1970 black education and wages have improved. During the first fifteen years of this century, the mortality rate for blacks and Hispanics

[4] Case and Deaton, *Deaths of Despair*, 3.
[5] Case and Deaton, *Deaths of Despair*, 7.
[6] Case and Deaton, *Deaths of Despair*, 7.
[7] Case and Deaton, *Deaths of Despair*, 178.

improved, while the mortality rate for uneducated, white, middle-aged men worsened.[8]

In the not so distant past, a factory worker or a tradesman of any race could support a family, maybe even buy a home, as my uncle did. But there have been huge changes in the American economy over the last several decades. A great deal of manufacturing has moved overseas, and trade school enrollment has declined because of declining blue-collar wages. After 1970, U.S. economic growth accelerated for the well-educated and already well-off, but stalled for the less educated and less well-off.[9] Whatever the reason my uncle felt such dissatisfaction with himself that he turned to drink, it seems that for many of today's working class men, a deep source of shame is having lost the economic well-being they once enjoyed in this country. Case and Deaton argue that while poverty matters, it is not poverty itself that leads to deaths of despair, but rather the long-term deterioration in opportunities for less-educated Americans.[10]

There are signs that the trend of diminishing opportunities for the working class could be slowly reversing: wages are improving in some sectors and new training programs are being developed to help workers transition to jobs with better prospects.[11] But not fast enough. Suicide rates increased 30 percent between 2000 and 2018. Suicide is one of the leading causes of death in the United States, with 45,979

[8] Case and Deaton, "Rising Morbidity and Mortality", 15079.

[9] Case and Deaton, *Deaths of Despair*, 149.

[10] Case and Deaton, *Deaths of Despair*, 144.

[11] See "Facing Skilled Worker Shortage, U.S. Companies Try to Train their Own New Labor Pools", *PBS News Hour*, July 1, 2021, pbs.org/newshour/education/facing-skilled-worker-shortage-u-s-companies-try-to-train-their-own-new-labor-pools

deaths in 2020. This is about one death every eleven minutes.[12] While suicide and alcohol related deaths represent the majority of deaths of despair, accidental drug overdose is the fastest growing of the three causes. The term "accidental" is a misnomer; while many who die of an opioid overdose did not intend to die, there is nothing unintentional about the sequence of events leading up to their death.

What was the impact of the COVID-19 pandemic on deaths of despair? During the pandemic, deaths from drug overdose increased significantly.[13] Surprisingly, despite the multitude of stressors created by the pandemic, death from suicide declined slightly (3 percent) in 2020 compared with prior years.[14] However, the slight decline in death by suicide was greatly overshadowed by the increases in drug overdose and alcoholic liver disease, resulting in a significant net increase in deaths of despair during the pandemic.

A death of despair is the antithesis of a good death. To die well, one must live well, and a life of addiction is undoubtedly not a life well lived. The fundamental problem driving an increase in deaths of despair is the decline in economic well-being of middle-aged white men. Lack of education or training and low income are two sides of the same coin. What, then, can be done? Or more specifically, what is the Catholic response?

[12] "Facts about Suicide," Centers for Disease Control and Prevention, last reviewed October 24, 2022, cdc.gov/suicide/facts.

[13] "U.S. Overdose Deaths In 2021 Increased Half as Much as in 2020—But Are Still Up 15%", Centers for Disease Control and Prevention, last reviewed April 26, 2023, cdc.gov/nchs/pressroom/nchs_press_releases/2022/202205.htm.

[14] Sally C. Curtin, Holly Hedegaard, and Farida B. Ahmad, "Provisional Numbers and Rates of Suicide by Month and Demographic Characteristics: United States, 2020" (NVSS Vital Statistics Rapid Release, report no. 16), November 2021, cdc.gov/nchs/data/vsrr/VSRR016.pdf.

The Catholic Church has consistently taught the importance of education, including vocational training. The Vatican II document *Gravissimum educationis* declared, "All men of every race, condition and age, since they enjoy the dignity of a human being, have an inalienable right to an education that is in keeping with their ultimate goal, their ability, their sex and the culture and tradition of their country."[15] The family has the primary responsibility for providing education, but schools have a special importance and Catholic schools even more so.

> The influence of the Church in the field of education is shown in a special manner by the Catholic school. No less than other schools does the Catholic school pursue cultural goals and the human formation of youth. But its proper function is to create for the school community a special atmosphere animated by the Gospel spirit of freedom and charity, to help youth grow according to the new creatures they were made through baptism as they develop their own personalities, and finally to order the whole of human culture to the news of salvation so that the knowledge the students gradually acquire of the world, life and man is illumined by faith.[16]

The document calls for schools of every kind—grammar schools, vocational schools, colleges and universities, schools for those with special needs, and ongoing education centers for adults—so that every person can develop to his full potential. Not only does the individual benefit from an education, but the Church and the society as a whole benefit from people pursuing knowledge developing their talents.

Providing education is not sufficient if it is not accessible

[15] Vatican Council II, Declaration on Christian Education *Gravissimum educationis* (October 28, 1965), no. 1.

[16] *Gravissimum educationis*, no. 8.

to all socioeconomic groups, and the Church has stressed the importance of making college readily available to qualified poor students who without financial help might be otherwise unable to afford it.[17] According to the Association of Catholic Colleges and Universities, there are 226 Catholic institutions participating in federal student financial aid programs, with about 850,000 enrolled students. For academic year 2017–2018, on average, 38 percent of full-time, first-time undergraduates at Catholic colleges and universities received Pell Grants, the federal need-based grants program for low-income students.

Suicide and Addiction

Suicide

While income disparity can be a contributing factor in deaths of despair, it is important to look at the specific manner in which people are dying. The problem of suicide is enormous. According to the CDC, in 2018 suicide was the tenth leading cause of death in the United States. That year, 48,344 people in the United States killed themselves.[18] Before we breeze past these statistics, let's take a closer look at some of the data. For individuals between the ages ten and thirty-four, suicide was the second leading cause of death, and for people between the ages of thirty-five and fifty-four, it was the third leading cause of death. Delving deeper, we find that *suicide was the second leading cause of death for children ages ten to fourteen* (accidental injury was the leading cause). Whether

[17] *Gravissimum educationis*, no. 10.
[18] The CDC WONDER website (https://wonder.cdc.gov/) is an online database and query system for the analysis of public health data. Data is updated regularly. For 2018, the ten leading causes of death were found at https://webappa.cdc.gov/cgi-bin/broker.exe, accessed January 29, 2021.

you were a tweener or a millennial, you were more likely to die from suicide than murder, cancer, heart disease, or infection. More details can be found on the CDC website, but the point is this: a staggering number of people kill themselves each year. The statistics are sobering.

In itself, suicide is a threat against the well-being of all, and for Catholics it is the antithesis of *Ars Moriendi*, the art of dying well. Those who commit suicide are *ipso facto* unwell intellectually, emotionally, and spiritually. One would think that given the scale of the problem, we would find an abundance of writings by Catholic theologians or magisterial documents regarding suicide. Unfortunately, this is not the case. Official Church teaching on suicide is relatively sparse.

Over the centuries, the Church's teaching on suicide has developed from what now sounds like a very harsh perspective to a more pastoral approach. While some of the Church Fathers, including Origen, Jerome, and Ambrose, condemned suicide, it was Augustine who first looked in depth at the morality of the act. In *The City of God*, Augustine states that suicide in all cases is wrong, as it is the deliberate destruction of innocent life. He interprets the fifth commandment, "Thou shall not kill", to include the killing of self and writes, "Christians have no authority for committing suicide in any circumstances whatever. . . . Truth plainly declares . . . that suicide is a detestable and damnable wickedness. . . . Those who die by their own hand have no better life after death."[19] Augustine leaves no doubt: suicide is wrong in all situations. The mental and emotional state of the person is not discussed.

[19] St. Augustine, *The City of God*, trans. Marcus Dodds, D.D. (New York: Modern Library), 2000, Book I, nos. 20, 25, and 26.

Aquinas likewise affirms that suicide is the destruction of innocent human life and a contradiction to justice, the common good, and self-love. For Aquinas, suicide is an act contrary to hope and the desire to seek out the good.[20]

G. K. Chesterton doubled down on the sinful nature of suicide: "Not only is suicide a sin, it is *the* sin. It is the ultimate and absolute evil, the refusal to take the oath of loyalty to life."[21] Suicide was not seen as a result of illness but a protest to God.

Pope Saint Paul VI touched briefly on the issue of suicide, including it in a list of threats against the dignity of life:

> Furthermore, whatever is opposed to life itself, such as any type of murder, genocide, abortion, euthanasia or *willful self-destruction*, whatever violates the integrity of the human person, such as mutilation, torments inflicted on body or mind, attempts to coerce the will itself; whatever insults human dignity, such as subhuman living conditions, arbitrary imprisonment, deportation, slavery, prostitution, the selling of women and children; as well as disgraceful working conditions, where men are treated as mere tools for profit, rather than as free and responsible persons; all these things and others of their like are infamies indeed. They poison human society, but they do more harm to those who practice them than those who suffer from the injury. Moreover, they are a supreme dishonor to the Creator.[22]

With time, however, clinicians gained a better understanding of the psychological dysfunction associated with suicide and the tone of Church teaching began to soften. In

---

[20] See Thomas Aquinas, *Summa Theologica* II-II, q. 64, art. 5.

[21] G. K. Chesterton, *Orthodoxy* (San Francisco: Ignatius Press, 1995), 78.

[22] Vatican Council II, Pastoral Constitution on the Church in the Modern World *Gaudium et spes* (December 7, 1965), no. 27, emphasis added.

1980, the Congregation for the Doctrine of the Faith stated that suicide and homicide are objectively morally equivalent, yet recognized that a person's personal moral responsibility could be reduced:

> Intentionally causing one's own death, or suicide, is therefore equally as wrong as murder; such an action on the part of a person is to be considered as a rejection of God's sovereignty and loving plan. Furthermore, suicide is also often a refusal of love for self, the denial of a natural instinct to live, a flight from the duties of justice and charity owed to one's neighbor, to various communities or to the whole of society—*although, as is generally recognized, at times there are psychological factors present that can diminish responsibility or even completely remove it.* However, one must clearly distinguish suicide from that sacrifice of one's life whereby for a higher cause, such as God's glory, the salvation of souls or the service of one's brethren, a person offers his or her own life or puts it in danger (cf. *Jn.* 15:14).[23]

In 1995, Pope Saint John Paul II affirmed this teaching in *Evangelium vitae*:

> Suicide is always as morally objectionable as murder. The Church's tradition has always rejected it as a gravely evil choice. Even though a certain psychological, cultural and social conditioning may induce a person to carry out an action which so radically contradicts the innate inclination to life, thus lessening or removing subjective responsibility, suicide, when viewed objectively, is a gravely immoral act. In fact, it involves the rejection of love of self and the renunciation of the obligation of justice and charity towards one's neighbour, towards the communities to which one belongs, and towards society as a whole. In its deepest

[23] Congregation for the Doctrine of the Faith, Declaration on Euthanasia *Iura et Bona* (May 5, 1980), no. 3, emphasis added.

reality, suicide represents a rejection of God's absolute sovereignty over life and death, as proclaimed in the prayer of the ancient sage of Israel: "You have power over life and death; you lead men down to the gates of Hades and back again" (Wis 16:13; cf. Tob 13:2).[24]

John Paul's tone seems a bit more pastoral than the 1980 statement by the CDF. He elaborates more on factors that may mitigate moral responsibility but again reiterates that the act of suicide is objectively gravely immoral.

In just a few paragraphs, the *Catechism of the Catholic Church* provides the most current magisterial teaching on suicide:

> Everyone is responsible for his life before God who has given it to him. It is God who remains the sovereign Master of life. We are obliged to accept life gratefully and preserve it for his honor and the salvation of our souls. We are stewards, not owners, of the life God has entrusted to us. It is not ours to dispose of.
>
> Suicide contradicts the natural inclination of the human being to preserve and perpetuate his life. It is gravely contrary to the just love of self. It likewise offends love of neighbor because it unjustly breaks the ties of solidarity with family, nation, and other human societies to which we continue to have obligations. Suicide is contrary to love for the living God.
>
> If suicide is committed with the intention of setting an example, especially to the young, it also takes on the gravity of scandal. Voluntary co-operation in suicide is contrary to the moral law. Grave psychological disturbances, anguish, or grave fear of hardship, suffering, or torture can diminish the responsibility of the one committing suicide.
>
> We should not despair of the eternal salvation of persons who have taken their own lives. By ways known to

[24] John Paul II, encyclical letter *Evangelium vitae* (The Gospel of Life) (March 25, 1995), no. 66.

him alone, God can provide the opportunity for salutary repentance. The Church prays for persons who have taken their own lives.[25]

Consistent with other Church documents, the *Catechism* stresses that suicide is an affront to the dignity afforded to all human life and is contrary to love of God. However, as do recent papal documents, it acknowledges that moral responsibility may be reduced under certain circumstances. The *Catechism* takes a pastoral tone one step further by warning against despair for the salvation of the deceased; God's ways are not our ways, and he alone is the judge.

Just as official teaching has struck a more pastoral tone over the years, so too has the position regarding funerals and burials for victims of suicide, but only in recent decades. By the end of the nineteenth century, most Western countries had decriminalized the act of suicide. However, the burial of someone who committed suicide was banned under the 1917 Code of Canon Law, which denied a Catholic burial to the unbaptized, the cremated, manifest sinners, and culpable suicides. For the funeral to be denied, the person who had committed suicide must have been deemed wholly responsible, and if there was any doubt about the deceased's state of mind, a private burial was allowed. If a Catholic funeral was denied, the deceased had to be buried outside consecrated ground, and it was forbidden to celebrate Mass on the anniversary of death.[26]

The 1983 Code of Canon Law, which is the current code, removed suicide from the list of reasons to deny a Catholic funeral. According to canon 1184, Christian burial is

[25] *CCC* 2280–83.

[26] Ranana Leigh Dine, "You Shall Bury Him: Burial, Suicide and the Development of Catholic Law and Theology", *Journal of Medical Humanities* 46, no. 3 (September 2020), 300.

denied only to "notorious apostates, heretics, schismatics, and those who choose cremation for reasons opposed to the Christian faith and other manifest sinners." In fact, not only is a funeral allowed for someone who committed suicide, a specific prayer is now said for the deceased:

> God, lover of souls, you hold dear what you have made and spare all things, for they are yours. Look gently on your servant N., and by the blood of the cross forgive his/her sins and failings. Remember the faith of those who mourn and satisfy their longing for that day when all will be made new again in Christ, our risen Lord, who lives and reigns with you forever and ever. Amen.[27]

As it says in the *Catechism*, we should not despair over the salvation of someone who commits suicide. Even though the act of suicide is without a doubt gravely morally wrong, the Lord knows the intention of our hearts, as well as our mental capacity and emotional stability. We can trust in his mercy and forgiveness and the hope of salvation from the one who sits on the throne and declares, "Behold, I make all things new" (Rev 21:5).

Addiction

According to the CDC, in 2019 nearly 71,000 people died of drug overdose, making it the leading cause of injury-related deaths. The CDC also reports that academic achievement is inversely related to the use of drugs: those with higher grades in school are less likely to use drugs.[28] Of the deaths

[27] International Commission on English in the Liturgy, *Order of Christian Funerals* (Totowa, N.J.: Catholic Book Publishing Co., 2019), 372.

[28] Centers for Disease Control and Prevention, "Making the Connection: Alcohol and Academic Grades" (DASH fact sheet), cdc.gov/healthy youth/health_and_academics/pdf/DASHFactSheetDrugUse.pdf.

from drug overdose in 2020, over 75 percent involved illicit or prescription opioid.[29] The term *opioids* is used for both natural derivatives of the opium poppy (codeine, morphine) and synthetically produced compounds that have the same properties (heroin, fentanyl, oxycodone, hydrocodone). Of these drugs, heroin is the only one that cannot be legally used with a prescription in the United States.

The "opioid crisis" has become front-page news in the past ten years. From 1999 to 2019, nearly 500,000 people died from an overdose involving an opioid. This rise in opioid overdose deaths occurred in three distinct waves. The first wave began with increased prescribing of opioids in the 1990s, with overdose deaths involving prescription opioids. The second wave began in 2010, with rapid increases in overdose deaths involving heroin. The third wave began in 2013, with significant increases in overdose deaths involving synthetic opioids, particularly those involving illicitly manufactured fentanyl. The market for illicitly manufactured fentanyl continues to change, and it can be found in combination with heroin, counterfeit pills, and cocaine.[30]

Fentanyl flows into the United States primarily from Mexico, but in recent years, China and India have emerged as additional sources of the potent opioid.[31] Fentanyl is distinguished from other opioids primarily by its potency but also because it is inexpensive to produce. According to the CDC,

[29] Centers for Disease Control and Prevention, "Opioid Basics", last reviewed May 23, 2022, cdc.gov/opioids/basics/index.html.

[30] Centers for Disease Control and Prevention, "Understanding the Opioid Overdose Epidemic", last reviewed June 1, 2022, cdc.gov/opioids/basics/epidemic.html.

[31] DEA Intelligence Program—Strategic Intelligence Section, "Fentanyl Flow to the United States" (DEA intelligence report), January 2020, dea.gov/sites/default/files/2020-03/DEA_GOV_DIR-008-20%20Fentanyl%20Flow%20in%20the%20United%20States_0.pdf.

fentanyl is up to fifty times stronger than heroin and one hundred times stronger than morphine.[32] Its potency and the lack of quality control in the black market make it easy to cause overdoses—including when users don't know that fentanyl is laced into or simply sold as other drugs. Powerful, often violent drug cartels in Mexico dominate the production and distribution of fentanyl.[33] Fentanyl is not only potentially lethal to the person using it, but the violence associated with the drug cartels adds even more victims. According to the Congressional Research Service, the Mexican government estimates about 15,000 Mexicans die each year in cartel-related homicides, and that number is likely much higher as many deaths go unreported. The cumulative total of Mexico's disappeared and missing reportedly exceeds 100,000 in 2022, with 90 percent of disappearances reported to have taken place since 2007.[34]

Deaths from opioid overdose occur within minutes, while deaths from alcohol-related liver disease occur over an extended period of time, months to years. Alcohol kills primarily from prolonged abuse that destroys the liver by the development of cirrhosis, a late-stage liver disease in which healthy liver tissue is replaced with scar tissue and the liver is permanently damaged. Binge drinking, consuming large amounts of alcohol in a short period of time, is more likely to cause cirrhosis than moderate daily drinking. Binge drink-

[32] Centers for Disease Control and Prevention, "Fentanyl Facts", last reviewed February 23, 2022, cdc.gov/stopoverdose/fentanyl.

[33] Jon Kamp, José de Córdoba, and Julie Wernau, "How Two Mexican Drug Cartels Came to Dominate America's Fentanyl Supply", *The Wall Street Journal*, Aug. 30, 2022, wsj.com/articles/mexico-drug-cartels-fentanyl-overdose-sinaloa-jalisco-11661866903.

[34] Congressional Research Service, "Mexico: Organized Crime and Drug Trafficking Organizations" (CRS report), updated June 7, 2022, sgp.fas.org/crs/row/R41576.pdf.

ing is more common in those with less education, placing them at higher risk for alcoholic liver disease and death.[35]

Addiction is the common link between opioid overdose and alcohol-related liver disease. What is the Catholic response? First of all, the Church recognizes the evil associated with the production of illicit drugs: the *Catechism* reads, "Clandestine production of and trafficking in drugs are scandalous practices. They constitute direct co-operation in evil, since they encourage people to practices gravely contrary to the moral law."[36] While the Church teaches that abuse of drugs and alcohol is contrary to the moral law,[37] it also acknowledges "the entire Catholic community must demonstrate Christ's own love in opening our arms and hearts to those suffering from addiction and in advocating effective, compassionate policies to turn the tide of addiction in this country."[38]

John Paul II stressed the importance of psychological and sociological determinants of drug use:

> Psychologists and sociologists believe that the first cause that drives young people and adults to the fatal experience of drugs is the absence of clear and convincing motivations in life. Indeed, the absence of reference points, the lack of values, the conviction that nothing makes sense, and that living is, therefore, not worthwhile, the tragic and distressing feeling of being people who walk, unknown in an absurd universe, may call some to look for an exasperated and desperate escape. Psychology experts also say that the cause

[35] Case and Deaton, *Deaths of Despair*, 106.

[36] *CCC* 2291.

[37] See *CCC* 2290.

[38] United States Catholic Conference, *New Slavery, New Freedom: A Pastoral Message on Substance Abuse* (Washington, D.C.: United States Catholic Conference, 2020), usccb.org/resources/new-slavery-new-freedom-pastoral-message-substance-abuse.

of the drug phenomenon is the feeling of loneliness and in-
communicability that unfortunately weighs on the entire
modern, noisy, and anonymous society, and even on the
family.[39]

He also emphasized the particular role the Church has in
dealing with drug addiction:

> The drug phenomenon is, indeed, a matter of great con-
> cern throughout the world, which requires serious study
> and the involvement of all actors in society. It is a wound
> inflicted on humanity that imprisons many people in a spi-
> ral of suffering and alienation and in the face of which the
> Church cannot remain indifferent. The Church has a spe-
> cial responsibility to deal with the scourge of drug addic-
> tion and all the social problems that arise from it, because
> She wants to help every human being to live in freedom
> before God in the world.[40]

In 2018, Pope Francis hosted a three-day conference enti-
tled Drugs and Addictions: an Obstacle to Integral Human
Development. In his closing address, Pope Francis described
drug addiction as "an open wound in our society; its victims, once ensnared, exchange their freedom for enslave-
ment to a dependency that we can define as chemical."[41]
He called those who produce and distribute drugs "dealers
of death". He called for "better coordination of policies
aimed at halting the growth of drug abuse and addictions
—isolated policies are of no use: it is a human problem,

[39] Pontifical Council for Health Pastoral Care, *Church: Drugs and Drug Addiction* (Vatican City: Libreria Editrice Vaticana, 2021), no. 35.

[40] Pontifical Council for Health Pastoral Care, *Church: Drugs and Drug Addiction*, no. 371.

[41] Francis, Address to Participants in the International Conference on Drugs
and Addictions: An Obstacle to Integral Human Development (December
1, 2018).

it is a social problem, everything must be interconnected—through the creation of networks of solidarity and closeness to those suffering from these pathologies."

Not only does the Church recognize the problem of addiction and offer its pastoral support, it has responded to the crisis of addiction in tangible ways. Catholic-sponsored addiction treatment centers can be found throughout the entire United States and many other countries. There are now countless Catholic-based addiction treatment centers that are directly affiliated with the Church and Church agencies (such as Catholic Charities) across the United States. These centers serve clients from all walks of life and religious affiliation and often regardless of ability to pay. These centers are a "boots on the ground" response to the crisis of addiction and are on the front lines in the battle against deaths of despair.

PART II
SPIRITUALITY

10

Dying Well

In my introduction I described the good death of my father-in-law, Mike Lewandowski.

Mike first became ill while on a trip to Minnesota to visit family. He was suddenly gasping for air with even the slightest exertion. His ankles swelled to twice their normal size. Labs were drawn at the local ER, and he was told point-blank: "Get back home, *now*." Within two days, Mike was admitted to the University of Nebraska Medical Center. A port was placed and chemotherapy initiated. Within a short time, it was readily apparent that a cure was not possible and death was inevitable. Mike went home to die.

My wife and children joined the rest of the family at Hotel Lewandowski for almost a month. I continued to work during the week and traveled to our hometown on weekends to be with everyone. The kids would play "restaurant" and charge their "customers" a few pennies for macaroni and hotdogs. They would walk to the park, where they would feed the ducks and play in the playground just as I did when I was their age. Their lives, and mine, went on in a quasi-normal way. They loved being with their cousins. Every night was a campout on the floor. But all this took place against the backdrop of Grandpa Lew slowly and gloriously transitioning from this life to the next. Mike's impending death, while incredibly sad, was a celebration of a lifetime of faith and love for Christ.

As death drew close, Mike was mostly confined to his bed. Shades were drawn, a small lamp shed a gentle glow on the room. Mostly his eyes were closed, but he was still there. There was very little conversation, only praying, singing, and the reading of Scripture. As I took my turn, I read aloud the story of Martha and Mary from Luke's Gospel. I did not think Mike was listening, but I kept reading anyway.

> Now as they went on their way, he entered a village; and a woman named Martha received him into her house. And she had a sister called Mary, who sat at the Lord's feet and listened to his teaching. But Martha was distracted with much serving; and she went to him and said, "Lord, do you not care that my sister has left me to serve alone? Tell her then to help me." But the Lord answered her, "Martha, Martha, you are anxious and troubled about many things; one thing is needful. Mary has chosen the good portion, which shall not be taken away from her." (10:38–42)

The quiet in the room was broken by Mike pumping his fist into the air and loudly proclaiming, "I'm with Mary! I'm with Mary!" Even on his deathbed, Mike wanted nothing more than to sit at the feet of the Master.

On his front door hung a plaque that told any visitor exactly how Mike thought: "As for me and my house, we will serve the Lord" (Josh 24:15). Mike's spiritual openness to serve the Lord did not go away as he died. He did not shut down, withdraw into himself. If anything, his desire to serve Christ by sharing him with others was even greater. His home on Louise Street in Grand Island, Nebraska, became the destination for friends and family on pilgrimage to pay honor to a truly holy man. By drawing near to him, they were drawing near to Christ himself. Mike's death was fitting to his life: a holy death for a holy man.

In his seventeenth-century devotional work *The Art of Dying Well*, Saint Robert Bellarmine states what should be self-evident: "He who lives well, will die well."[1] Furthermore, to die well requires us to die to the world so that we may live for God. The essence of the good life is to cultivate the theological virtues of faith, hope, and charity, which are given to us at Baptism. To live well and die well, we must be obedient to God—and repent from disobedience. We should detach ourselves from worldly riches, avoid "ungodliness", show justice, and live a temperate life. To die well, we should make ourselves ready to meet Christ by growing close to him through prayer, fasting, and almsgiving. Small wonder that Mike died so well.

Mike's funeral was . . . I struggle to find the right adjective. It was one of the spiritual highlights of my life. The entire Lewandowski clan entered the cathedral and walked down the center aisle behind Mike's coffin. The church was packed. The altar was lined with priests who came to celebrate the funeral of a simple telephone repairman. The entire congregation was on their feet, hands upraised, loudly proclaiming as they sang "How Great Thou Art". The celebrant said that Mike didn't want the homily to be about him: "Only preach Jesus. Don't talk about me." The priest mostly followed Mike's request, but he began his homily with the obvious observation: "When you talk about Mike, you are talking about Jesus."

So, Mike is my model for how to die well, because he is my model for how to live well.

---

[1] Robert Bellarmine, *The Art of Dying Well*, trans. Rev. John Dalton (London: Richardson and Son, 1847), 2.

11

Dying to the World

Mary Ann could not sin. For four years or so, her cognitive function had deteriorated at the glacier-like speed typical of most dementias, punctuated by episodic precipitous declines from which she never fully recovered. Sometimes the downhill, stair-step course was marked by long plateaus of relatively stable function; at other times only a few weeks separated one sudden worsening from the next.

To commit a sin, a person must have full understanding of his actions and motives. By this point, Mary Ann had neither. While still cognizant, she frequented the sacrament of Confession. With time, it was no longer necessary to do so. Some might say she had regressed to a childlike existence, but nothing could be further from the truth. Despite the loss of memory and lack of full understanding of her surroundings, Mary Ann remained a spiritual treasure trove. A lifetime of fidelity to the Trinity had fueled a once-roaring flame. Though now subdued to glowing embers, it still exuded love. She was being purified, and people noticed her purity. "Blessed are the pure in heart, for they shall see God" (Mt 5:8).

This is a sacred time—the transition between full awareness and unresponsiveness. It is a time not to be rushed. It is a time to savor.

In the eyes of the world, Mary Ann's looming death was the antithesis of a good death. After all, she was confined to

137

a wheelchair, spent much of her day sleeping, and had only the faintest awareness of her surroundings. How could this be a good death?

In his book *The Art of Dying Well*, Saint Robert Bellarmine begins with the following:

> I now commence the rules to be observed in the art of dying well. . . . But the general rule, "that he who lives well, will die well," must be mentioned before all others: for since death is nothing more than the end of life, it is certain that all who live well to the end, die well; nor can he die ill, who hath never lived ill; as on the other hand, he who hath never led a good life, cannot die a good death.[1]

The basic premise that someone who lives a good life tends to die a good death seems self-evident. But the measure of a good death is not the same as the measure of an easy death. After all, the holiest of people can sometimes experience the most miserable of deaths. The list of Christian martyrs begins with the stoning of Saint Stephen and has continued ever since. Hundreds of martyr saints have been recognized over the centuries, and no doubt there are innumerable additional unrecognized martyrs.

So all this raises the question: What does it mean to die well? A peaceful, pain-free death surrounded by friends and family is certainly desirable, and supporters of assisted suicide and euthanasia would have us believe this type of death is the ideal way to die and the measure of a good death. But the implication is that a different kind of death, one marked by suffering or loneliness, is necessarily a bad death.

Of course we know this not to be true. The death of Jesus was necessary for the redemption of sin: "God shows his love for us in that while we were yet sinners Christ died

---

[1] Bellarmine, *The Art of Dying Well*, 1–2.

for us" (Rom 5:8). Christ's death was the good death *par excellence*, yet he suffered in every way imaginable and was abandoned by all save a handful of women and John the apostle.

So, if the absence of pain and suffering is not the measure of a good death, then what is?

Mary Ann had never been attached to material things, both by nature and by necessity. Along with her husband, Mike, she raised seven children on the wages of a telephone repairman. The house was always clean, and food was never lacking. Powdered milk helped stretch the fresh gallon. Iron-on patches healed the tattered knees of hand-me-down Levi's. Like so many others, Mary Ann learned to make do with what she had. But there was no wistfulness for nicer stuff. There was a contentment born out of a detachment from worldly things.

Throughout Scripture we find passages that encourage detachment. John the Evangelist tells us: "Do not love the world or the things in the world. If any one loves the world, love for the Father is not in him. For all that is in the world, the lust of the flesh and the lust of the eyes and the pride of life, is not of the Father but is of the world. And the world passes away, and the lust of it; but he who does the will of God abides for ever" (1 Jn 2:15–17). The majority of the stuff we own is neither good nor bad. It is just stuff. As Saint John of the Cross wrote, "Since the things of the world cannot enter the soul, they are not in themselves an encumbrance or harm to it; rather, it is the will and appetite dwelling within that cause the damage [when set on these things]."[2]

---

[2] John of the Cross, *The Ascent of Mount Carmel*, in *The Collected Works of St. John of the Cross*, trans. Kieran Kavanaugh and Otilio Rodriguez (Washington, D.C.: ICS Publications, 1973), 77.

It is not the thing; it is the attachment to the thing that weighs down the soul. What matters is not the things of the world but love for the Father. Many of the saints emphasize this point. In the *Spiritual Exercises*, Saint Ignatius describes holy indifference: "Therefore, we must make ourselves indifferent to all created things, as far as we are allowed by free choice and are not under any prohibition. Consequently, as far as we are concerned, we should not prefer health to sickness, riches to poverty, honor to dishonor, a long life to a short. The same holds for all other things."[3]

To die well is to let go of the things of this world and to abandon ourselves to love. For some, abandoning themselves into the source of love itself is a simple act of the will. For others, this decision is more difficult. Saint Robert Bellarmine continues: "We showed, that no one can die a good death, without first dying to the world. Now we shall point out what he must *do* who is dead to the world, in order that he may live to God; for . . . we proved, that no man can die well, without having lived well."[4]

As Mary Ann declined over the years, her meager material possessions were whittled away even further, so that by the time she was near death, all she had left were a few clothes, some pictures and other keepsakes, her rosary, and her deceased husband's Bible. COVID restrictions at her facility isolated her from family, and she spent more and more time alone. She was stripped of everything: her possessions, her mind, even her family. Yet she died a very, very good death.

As the end of life approached, family was once again allowed to visit. Periods of smiling wakefulness were increasingly replaced by sleep. Judicious doses of morphine helped

[3] Ignatius of Loyola, *Spiritual Exercises and Selected Works*, ed. George Ganss, S.J. (New York: Paulist Press 1991), 130.
[4] Bellarmine, *Art of Dying Well*, 12.

ease her pain but precipitated even more somnolence. Once she was no longer able to eat or drink, death was imminent. Small groups of family huddled at her bedside, whispering decade after decade of the Rosary. With family beside her, she breathed her last literally seconds after the final decade of the Glorious Mysteries was recited. A good death indeed.

12

What Comes Next

Fr. Pat had no legs, sort of. Actually, as a complication of diabetes and kidney failure, he endured amputations of both lower legs and used a motorized scooter to move about. Most priests in his condition would see retirement as a much-deserved respite in reward for a lifetime of service to the Church. Not Fr. Pat. He was never busier. Why? Because he was holy.

Like moths to a flame or iron to a magnet, people were drawn to Fr. Pat by his holiness. Devoid of an ounce of hubris, he had a self-deprecating Irish wit that was a thin veneer over what lay beneath: a deep-seated confidence that he was a beloved son of the Father.

One day, out of the blue, he said quite bluntly, "I want you to be there when I'm dying. I want you to help me make decisions." I was startled by the request, not because I thought I was unqualified, but because I thought I was undeserving. Birth and death are two of the most holy moments in a lifetime (if not *the* most holy), and to be invited into that time was an honor that humbled me deeply. Many people loved Fr. Pat and had known him longer and by all rights were more deserving. I accepted his precious request and asked him to let his family know of his wishes.

Fr. Pat's robust exterior appearance betrayed the hidden fragility of his health. Thrice-weekly dialysis meant waking at dawn and driving his handicap-accessible van to the center where he was tethered for hours to a machine that scrubbed the toxins from his blood that his failed kidneys could not metabolize. Congestive heart failure was a constant looming threat, and his lungs teetered between a satisfying full inspiration and a choking gasp. In the years I knew him, Fr. Pat had been hospitalized a number of times for exacerbations of his underlying chronic illnesses, but there never seemed to be an urgent sense that *now* was the time.

As the COVID pandemic raged, I worried for Fr. Pat. His need for dialysis demanded that he venture out into the community, putting his health at grave risk. Fortunately, he dodged the bullets of the COVID surges, and as the curve flattened, I thought less about the possibility that he would become yet another person with "high-risk medical conditions" who died of the virus.

At 11 P.M. I received a call to my cell phone: "Is this Dr. Doran?" I was irritated at first. I was not on call, and any calls from the hospital usually go through the answering service. No doubt my tone was abrupt: "Who is this?" It was Fr. Pat's sister. My irritability quickly gave way to concern as she informed me that he was hospitalized and on the verge of being placed on a ventilator. "Can you come right away?" Of course.

I arrived at Fr. Pat's bedside and could tell immediately that things did not look good. During the COVID pandemic, patients in the ICU could only have one visitor unless they were actively dying. Fr. Pat had seven. The pulmonologist at the bedside gave a quick sketch of his condition: blood pH excessively low, CO_2 levels excessively high, O_2 levels fluctuating wildly. Fr. Pat was wearing a BiPAP mask: air was being pushed into his lungs with each inspiration. In spite of this machine, fluid buildup in his lungs prevented adequate exchange of oxygen and carbon dioxide. Unless a breathing tube was placed and mechanical ventilation initiated, Fr. Pat would likely continue to decline, resulting in what is known as "multisystem organ failure". In short, without a ventilator, Fr. Pat would likely die very soon.

Months previously, Fr. Pat had anticipated this scenario. Given the number and severity of his underlying medical conditions, it would be difficult, maybe impossible, to wean him off the ventilator once it was started. He had made his wishes known clearly in advance. He did not want treatment that he considered excessively burdensome; that is, he did not want to receive painful care that had little chance of success. He would consent to ordinary treatment, but he would decline extraordinary treatment. In Fr. Pat's case, inserting a breathing tube into his lungs and placing him on a ventilator would be burdensome and extraordinary.

With the BiPAP mask in place and air being forced into his mouth and lungs, it was very difficult to hear Fr. Pat's words. I leaned in close, my face an inch from his. Some of the air from the BiPAP machine would leak around the edges of the mask and blow into my face; I felt as if I were in the midst of a prairie windstorm. In spite of his dire condition, Fr. Pat remained lucid and wanted my counsel: "Would it be okay if I said no to the ventilator?"

As a priest, Fr. Pat was well versed in Catholic moral theology, and he knew that under these circumstances, a decision to decline the ventilator would be morally acceptable. But having me at the bedside to confirm what he already knew was a comfort. I was his friend and understood both his medical condition and the teachings of the Church. "Yes, Fr. Pat. It is okay to say no." That was the extent of our conversation. Nothing more needed to be said.

I opened my Bible and read John, chapter 14, into his left ear. With the rushing air surrounding us, I began, "Let not your hearts be troubled; believe in God, believe also in me. In my Father's house are many rooms; if it were not so, would I have told you that I go to prepare a place for you? And when I go and prepare a place for you, I will come again and will take you to myself, that where I am you may be also" (Jn 14:1–3).

Fr. Pat was clearly suffering. The mask with its forced air was incredibly uncomfortable. He fidgeted with back pain. I held his left hand and continued to pray in his ear. I then had the audacity to ask him for a favor: "Would you pray for my son?" I knew "the prayer of a righteous man has great power in its effects" (Jas 5:16), and I reasoned the prayer of a righteous man so close to meeting Jesus would be exceptionally powerful in its effects.

"Of course I will." With that, I drew back to the corner of the room, giving others the opportunity to come close to holiness. A fellow priest arrived, and we were briefly ushered out of the room while Fr. Pat confessed his sins. After the Sacrament of Reconciliation, we were all invited back into the room to celebrate the Anointing of the Sick, ending with the Apostolic Pardon. I sat quietly in the corner while family surrounded his bed. I left about 2 A.M., knowing that Fr. Pat was in good hands.

I returned around 6 A.M., and he looked even worse. He was barely conscious, and I thought for sure that death was imminent. Others had also gone home, with plans to return after some rest. His brother-in-law was keeping solo vigil. We visited briefly. I received an update from his nurse, and I continued with rounding on my own patients, with a full clinic waiting to begin at 8 A.M.

As the day went on, I heard nothing more of his condition. I expected that he had died and his family had gone home. Later that afternoon, I called the nursing station, anticipating that his bed would be empty. Much to my surprise (and that is an understatement), the nurse told me Fr. Pat was sitting up in bed, eating and drinking. He no longer was "imminently dying", and visiting restrictions were back in place. Only one person and only family. I talked with him by phone the next day, and he seemed his usual self. Within a few days, his condition had improved further and he was sent home. Fr. Lazarus indeed.

A few weeks later, we gathered together via video conference to reflect on his "near-death" experience. "It was everything I hoped it would be", said Fr. Pat. What had he hoped for? To say goodbye to his family, to have a priest at his side, to receive the Sacrament of the Anointing of the Sick and the Apostolic Pardon, to make a general confession. All these desires were fulfilled that night. Fr. Pat also recalled being profoundly aware of the prayers being said for him at that moment: "I was at the center of all those prayers, and I could hear them praying and interceding on my behalf. It was beautiful!" Knowing that death was near, he was at peace. "It was magnificent; I was knocking on the door; I was ready to go. I was approaching death with eyes wide open, and I was not afraid." On top of all that, "the great torment that Satan sometimes throws at me wasn't there." A nagging doubt that had plagued him in recent years was gone, just when it might have been at its greatest.

And what was that great torment? "There is nothing after death. Just great nothingness." Especially in the isolation of the COVID pandemic, Fr. Pat's mind and spirit were assaulted with the possibility that death is the end of all existence, and that this would negate his entire life as a priest. If no heaven, then no God. "Satan would keep throwing this at me, and throwing it at me, and throwing it at me . . ." God seemed very far away. Yet the priest never gave himself over to despair; he was able to quell the temptations.

Fr. Pat nearly died the "perfect death", or at least the

death he had hoped for. He was comforted by the assurance that there is *something* after we die. And what is that something? The Four Last Things. For centuries, Christian tradition has taught that every man must face death, judgment, and heaven or hell.[1]

Death

The existence of the first of the Four Last Things seems readily apparent: death is inevitable. We all know that every living thing eventually dies. From the mayfly, which lives only about twenty-four hours, to the Greenland shark, which lives more than two hundred years, death eventually comes for all. As Saint Paul says, creation is "subjected to futility" (Rom 8:20), but in the beginning, this was not so.

When God created mankind, he intended for Adam and Eve to live forever. "As long as he remained in the divine intimacy, man would not have to suffer or die."[2] But with the disobedience of Adam and Eve, sin entered the world, and

---

[1] The doctrine of purgatory is traditionally not included in the Four Last Things. Catholic teaching on purgatory is summarized in the *Catechism of the Catholic Church*: "All who die in God's grace and friendship, but still imperfectly purified, are indeed assured of their eternal salvation; but after death they undergo purification, so as to achieve the holiness necessary to enter the joy of heaven" (*CCC* 1030); "The Church gives the name *Purgatory* to this final purification of the elect, which is entirely different from the punishment of the damned. The Church formulated her doctrine of faith on Purgatory especially at the Councils of Florence and Trent. The tradition of the Church, by reference to certain texts of Scripture, speaks of a cleansing fire" (*CCC* 1031); "This teaching is also based on the practice of prayer for the dead, already mentioned in Sacred Scripture: 'Therefore [Judas Maccabeus] made atonement for the dead, that they might be delivered from their sin.' From the beginning the Church has honored the memory of the dead and offered prayers in suffrage for them, above all the Eucharistic sacrifice, so that, thus purified, they may attain the beatific vision of God. The Church also commends almsgiving, indulgences, and works of penance undertaken on behalf of the dead" (*CCC* 1032).

[2] *CCC* 376.

with sin came death. Original sin is an essential truth of the faith: "a primeval event, a deed that took *place at the beginning of the history of man*. Revelation gives us the certainty of faith that the whole of human history is marked by the original fault freely committed by our first parents."[3] Thus Saint Paul says, "Therefore as sin came into the world through one man and death through sin, and so death spread to all men because all men sinned" (Rom 5:12). Saint Augustine adds, "Sin is the father of death. If there had been no sin, there would have been no death."[4]

The *Catechism* teaches that although death is the end of earthly life, a consequence of sin, it is transformed by Christ.[5] Joseph Cardinal Ratzinger, before he became Pope Benedict, said that death can be best interpreted through the message of the Cross:

> That message interprets death by teaching us to see in dying more than the end point of biological existence. . . . Death is present in the nothingness of an empty existence which ends up in a mere semblance of living. Secondly, death is present as the physical process of disintegration which accompanies life. . . . Thirdly, death is met with the daring of that love which leaves self behind, giving itself to the other.[6]

He went on to say, "The Christian dies into the death of Christ himself. . . . Death is vanquished where people die with Christ and into him. This is why the Christian attitude must be opposed to the modern wish for instantaneous death, a wish that would turn death into an extensionless

[3] *CCC* 390

[4] Augustine, *Sermons of the Liturgical Season*, 231.2, quoted in Edward Condon, *Death, Judgment, Heaven and Hell: Sayings of the Fathers of the Church* (Washington, D.C.: Catholic University Press of America, 2019), 2.

[5] *CCC* 1007–9.

[6] Joseph Ratzinger, *Eschatology: Death and Eternal Life*, 2nd ed. (Washington, D.C.: Catholic University Press of America, 1988), 95.

moment and banish from life the claims of the metaphysical."[7] Death is much more than the inevitable end of earthly existence.

Judgment

If death is inevitable, what then of judgment, the second of the Four Last Things? After we die, will we be judged? Jesus makes a number of references to judgment, among them: "I tell you, on the day of judgment men will render account for every careless word they utter; for by your words you will be justified, and by your words you will be condemned" (Mt 12:36–37); "When the Son of man comes in his glory, and all the angels with him, then he will sit on his glorious throne. Before him will be gathered all the nations, and he will separate them one from another as a shepherd separates the sheep from the goats" (Mt 25:31–32). Saint Paul states quite plainly, "For we must all appear before the judgment seat of Christ, so that each one may receive good or evil, according to what he has done in the body" (2 Cor 5:10). The Letter to the Hebrews tells us, "It is appointed for men to die once, and after that comes judgment" (9:27).

So what is meant exactly by judgment? Who is the judge and what is being judged? The Gospel of John makes it clear that Jesus is the judge: "The Father judges no one, but has given all judgment to the Son . . . and has given him authority to execute judgment" (Jn 5:22, 27). As just mentioned, Paul tells us we will appear before the judgment seat of Christ. The "who" of judgment is obvious; how about the "what"?

Particular Judgment

From its earliest times, the Church has taught the particular judgment, which each individual will receive after death.

[7] Ratzinger, *Eschatology*, 97.

According to Origen, "An account is to be drawn up for each of us. There is no other time to give an account except the time of judgment. Then, what is entrusted to us, and what gains or losses we have made, will be clearly known."[8] The *Catechism of the Catholic Church* gives the following description of the particular judgment:

> Death puts an end to human life as the time open to either accepting or rejecting the divine grace manifested in Christ. The New Testament speaks of judgment primarily in its aspect of the final encounter with Christ in his second coming, but also repeatedly affirms that each will be rewarded immediately after death in accordance with his works and faith. The parable of the poor man Lazarus and the words of Christ on the cross to the good thief, as well as other New Testament texts speak of a final destiny of the soul—a destiny which can be different for some and for others.
>
> Each man receives his eternal retribution in his immortal soul at the very moment of his death, in a particular judgment that refers his life to Christ: either entrance into the blessedness of heaven—through a purification or immediately,—or immediate and everlasting damnation.[9]

In simple terms, the particular judgment of a person has two elements: the actions I have done or not done during my life, and the consequences of these actions. The judgment of our actions is a judgment between good or evil, virtue or vice, merit or sin.

> Sin is an offense against reason, truth, and right conscience; it is failure in genuine love for God and neighbor caused by a perverse attachment to certain goods. It wounds the

---

[8] Origen, *Homilies on Luke*, 35.11, quoted in Condon, *Death, Judgment, Heaven and Hell*, 27.

[9] *CCC* 1021–22.

nature of man and injures human solidarity. It has been defined as an utterance, a deed, or a desire contrary to the
eternal law.

Sin is an offense against God. . . . Sin sets itself against
God's love for us and turns our hearts away from it. Like
the first sin, it is disobedience, a revolt against God through
the will to become "like gods," knowing and determining
good and evil. Sin is thus "love of oneself even to contempt
of God." In this proud self-exaltation, sin is diametrically
opposed to the obedience of Jesus, which achieves our salvation.[10]

Whether a given action is morally wrong depends on what
are known as the moral determinants: (1) the object chosen,
(2) the end in view or the intention, and (3) the circumstances of the action. The object chosen is the action itself;
for a given action to be morally acceptable, the action itself
must be morally good, or at least neutral. The intention of
a person can determine whether a particular action is good
or bad. The action and intention are the primary elements
of a moral act, while the circumstances are secondary. They
can either increase or decrease the moral goodness or evil of
a particular act, and they can also diminish or increase the
person's responsibility.

Some actions in themselves are always morally wrong.
They violate the natural law, the law of God written on
our hearts. That is, they are intrinsically evil. Quoting the
Second Vatican Council, Pope Saint John Paul II states:

Whatever is hostile to life itself, such as any kind of homicide, genocide, abortion, euthanasia and voluntary suicide;
whatever violates the integrity of the human person, such
as mutilation, physical and mental torture and attempts to
coerce the spirit; whatever is offensive to human dignity,
such as subhuman living conditions, arbitrary imprison-

[10] CCC 1849–50.

ment, deportation, slavery, prostitution and trafficking in women and children; degrading conditions of work which treat labourers as mere instruments of profit, and not as free responsible persons: all these and the like are a disgrace, and so long as they infect human civilization they contaminate those who inflict them more than those who suffer injustice, and they are a negation of the honour due to the Creator.[11]

Intrinsically evil acts are always evil, regardless of the circumstances. While a person's moral responsibility may be reduced in certain circumstances, the action itself remains morally wrong.

So while this detailed discussion on what constitutes sin is relevant, we return to the starting premise on judgment: Jesus Christ is the judge. While the Church has many times declared who *is* in heaven (that is, the saints), the Church has never declared who *is not* in heaven. We can and do make judgments on the morality of people's actions, and our legal system assigns various degrees of responsibility for illegal actions; but whether or not God assigns a particular soul to "everlasting damnation" is not ours to say.

General Judgment

"He will come again in glory to judge the living and the dead." These words roll off our tongues every Sunday when we profess the Nicene Creed, and yet how many Catholics believe what they say? As it turns out, a majority of Catholics believe in the Second Coming of Christ. According to the Pew Research Center, approximately 70 percent of Catholics

[11] Vatican Council II, Pastoral Constitution on the Church in the Modern World *Gaudium et spes* (December 7, 1965), no. 27, quoted in John Paul II, encyclical letter *Veritatis splendor* (The Splendor of Truth) (August 6, 1993), no. 80.

believe that Jesus will at some point return to earth,[12] and about a third of Catholics believe he will do so by the year 2050.[13]

The general judgment is also known as the Last Judgment:

> The resurrection of all the dead, "of both the just and the unjust" [Acts 24:15], will precede the Last Judgment. This will be "the hour when all who are in the tombs will hear [the Son of man's] voice and come forth, those who have done good, to the resurrection of life, and those who have done evil, to the resurrection of judgment" [Jn 5:28–29]. Then Christ will come "in his glory, and all the angels with him. . . . Before him will be gathered all the nations, and he will separate them one from another as a shepherd separates the sheep from the goats, and he will place the sheep at his right hand, but the goats at the left. . . . And they will go away into eternal punishment, but the righteous into eternal life" [Mt 25:31, 32, 46].[14]

> The Last Judgment will come when Christ returns in glory. Only the Father knows the day and the hour; only he determines the moment of its coming. Then through his Son Jesus Christ he will pronounce the final word on all history. We shall know the ultimate meaning of the whole work of creation and of the entire economy of salvation and understand the marvellous ways by which his Providence led everything towards its final end. The Last Judgment will reveal that God's justice triumphs over all the injustices committed by his creatures and that God's love is stronger than death.[15]

From its earliest days, Church tradition has taught that there will be a final judgment and that it will be accompa-

---

[12] "Many Americans Uneasy with Mix of Religion and Politics: Section IV—Religious Beliefs" (report), Pew Research Center, August 24, 2006, pewresearch.org/politics/2006/08/24/section-iv-religious-beliefs/.

[13] "Jesus Christ's Return to Earth", Pew Research Center, July 14, 2020, pewresearch.org/fact-tank/2010/07/14/jesus-christs-return-to-earth/.

[14] CCC 1038.

[15] CCC 1040.

nied by the resurrection of the dead. If death is the unnatural division of the body and soul, the resurrection of the body is the event that returns us to our natural state. As Saint Augustine says, "Scripture teaches us two things: first, that judgment will come; second, that it will be accompanied by the resurrection of the dead. John the Evangelist tells us with perfect plainness that Christ foretold that judgment was to come at the time of the resurrection of the dead."[16]

In the First Letter to the Corinthians, Saint Paul gives an extended discussion on the resurrection of the body, connecting it with the Resurrection of Jesus.

> Now if Christ is preached as raised from the dead, how can some of you say that there is no resurrection of the dead? But if there is no resurrection of the dead, then Christ has not been raised; if Christ has not been raised, then our preaching is in vain and your faith is in vain. . . . But in fact Christ has been raised from the dead, the first fruits of those who have fallen asleep. (15:12–14, 20)

The resurrection of the dead is a very evocative image, and in Matthew's Gospel, we see a foreshadowing of this event. Just after Jesus gives over his spirit on the cross, "the curtain of the temple was torn in two, from top to bottom; and the earth shook, and the rocks were split; the tombs also were opened, and many bodies of the saints who had fallen asleep were raised, and coming out of the tombs after his resurrection they went into the holy city and appeared to many" (27:51–53).

What will be the nature of our resurrected bodies? Scripture gives us some hints. After the Resurrection, Jesus appeared to his followers on many occasions, and the common theme of these events is that people initially did not

---

[16] Augustine, *City of God*, 20.5, quoted in Condon, *Death, Judgment, Heaven and Hell*, 29.

recognize him. Mary Magdalene did not recognize the resurrected Jesus in the garden until he spoke her name (cf. Jn 20:11–18). The disciples on the road to Emmaus did not realize it was Jesus walking with them and explaining the scriptures until he broke bread with them (cf. Lk 24:13–35). Peter recognized Jesus on the shore of the Sea of Galilee only after Jesus instructed him to cast out his nets again, catching an enormous amount of fish (cf. Jn 21).

So, it seems our resurrected bodies will be somehow different yet at the same time similar to our earthly bodies. Saint Paul describes the difference between our physical and spiritual bodies.

> But some one will ask, "How are the dead raised? With what kind of body do they come?" You foolish man! What you sow does not come to life unless it dies. And what you sow is not the body which is to be, but a bare kernel, perhaps of wheat or of some other grain. . . . So is it with the resurrection of the dead. What is sown is perishable, what is raised is imperishable. It is sown in dishonor, it is raised in glory. It is sown in weakness, it is raised in power. It is sown a physical body, it is raised a spiritual body. If there is a physical body, there is also a spiritual body. (1 Cor 15:35–37, 42–44)

Likewise, the Assumption of Mary into heaven points toward our own bodily resurrections. While Scripture does not explicitly tell of this event, sacred tradition has long held that when her mission on earth was complete, Mary was assumed body and soul into heaven.

> "Finally the Immaculate Virgin, preserved free from all stain of original sin, when the course of her earthly life was finished, was taken up body and soul into heavenly glory, and exalted by the Lord as Queen over all things, so that she might be the more fully conformed to her Son, the Lord of lords and conqueror of sin and death." [*Lumen gentium*,

no. 59] The Assumption of the Blessed Virgin is a singular participation in her Son's Resurrection and an anticipation of the resurrection of other Christians.[17]

Heaven

Pop culture is obsessed with heaven. From movies (*Heaven Is for Real, All Dogs Go to Heaven, Heaven Can Wait*) to songs ("Stairway to Heaven", "Knockin' on Heaven's Door", "Heaven on My Mind"), what comes next continues to fascinate and inspire. Mention the word *heaven* to an average person and this will conjure up images of fluffy white clouds, winged angels with harps, brilliant rays of sunshine, and so on. Peace, joy, bliss—as cliché as it is, this notion of heaven points toward what Catholics believe about heaven: union with God is our greatest happiness, true beatitude.

A quick sidebar on the word *heaven* as it appears in the Bible: In some cases, heaven refers to the created sky above or, in more technical terms, the atmosphere of the earth: "In the beginning God created the heavens and the earth" (Gen 1:1); "When I look at your heavens, the work of your fingers, the moon and the stars which you have established; what is man that you are mindful of him, and the son of man that you care for him?" (Ps 8:3–4). In other passages, heaven refers to the dwelling place of God: "And whenever you stand praying, forgive, if you have anything against any one; so that your Father also who is in heaven may forgive you your trespasses" (Mk 11:25); "The LORD looks down from heaven upon the children of men, to see if there are any that act wisely, that seek after God" (Ps 14:2).

The final destination of our spiritual journey is meant to be union with God, which is heaven. Saints such as Teresa

[17] *CCC* 966.

of Ávila and John of the Cross describe the spiritual life as a series of steps, beginning with the Purgative Way, which is turning away from sin. From there, the journey continues through the Illuminative Way and the Unitive Way, whereby the person grows in virtue and love for God. The spiritual journey reaches its final intended destination in the Beatific Vision: "Because of his transcendence, God cannot be seen as he is, unless he himself opens up his mystery to man's immediate contemplation and gives him the capacity for it. The Church calls this contemplation of God in his heavenly glory 'the beatific vision.'"[18]

Then-Cardinal Ratzinger states that heaven can only be understood in the reality of Christ: "Heaven's existence depends on the fact that Jesus Christ, as God, is man and makes space for human existence in the existence of God himself. One is in heaven when, and to the degree, that one is in Christ."[19] The future Pope Benedict echoes the words of the saints. Heaven is union with God. Salvation, properly understood, is only fully realized in heaven. It is true that Christ "saves" us through his death and Resurrection, and while we might be "saved" while still alive, our salvation lies in heaven, our final destination, the fulfillment of our deepest longings.

Since our final destination is reached only after death, we can only imagine what heaven is like. This, of course, leads to an abundance of questions and speculation, some profound and sublime, some trivial and banal, ranging from "Will my dog be with me in heaven?" to "Will I be truly happy if my children are not with me in heaven?" The list is endless.

The Nicene Creed mentions heaven twice: "For us men

[18] *CCC* 1028.
[19] Ratzinger, *Eschatology*, 236.

and for our salvation He came down from heaven. . . . He ascended into heaven and is seated at the right hand of the Father." So when we recite the Creed, we are at least indirectly affirming the existence of heaven. According to the most recent Pew Research Center survey, 90 percent of U.S. Catholics say they believe in heaven.[20] While almost all Catholics agree that heaven exists, what they think heaven is like is more variable. The majority of Christians believe that in heaven, people are free of suffering, meet God, and are reunited with loved ones who have previously died. A smaller number believe that people in heaven are reunited with pets or animals they knew on earth, or that people in heaven can see what is happening on earth.

Like many things, what heaven is like remains a mystery until we die. Even Lazarus, whom Jesus brought back to life after three days in the tomb, does not give us a hint. "This mystery of blessed communion with God and all who are in Christ is beyond all understanding and description. Scripture speaks of it in images: life, light, peace, wedding feast, wine of the kingdom, the Father's house, the heavenly Jerusalem, paradise: 'no eye has seen, nor ear heard, nor the heart of man conceived, what God has prepared for those who love him' [1 Cor 2:9]."[21]

Hell

The same questions about heaven can be asked about hell: whether it exists, what it is like, and so on. While the vast majority of Catholics believe in the existence of heaven,

---

[20] "Views on the Afterlife: Majorities of U.S. Adults Say They Believe in Heaven, Hell", Pew Research Center, November 23, 2021, pewresearch.org/religion/2021/11/23/views-on-the-afterlife/.

[21] *CCC* 1027.

they are not so sure about hell: 90 percent versus 74 percent.[22] The Church confirms that there is indeed a hell: "The teaching of the Church affirms the existence of hell and its eternity. Immediately after death the souls of those who die in a state of mortal sin descend into hell, where they suffer the punishments of hell, 'eternal fire.' The chief punishment of hell is eternal separation from God, in whom alone man can possess the life and happiness for which he was created and for which he longs."[23]

Interestingly, unlike heaven, hell is not mentioned in the Nicene Creed. However, the Apostles' Creed mentions hell: "He (Jesus) descended into hell; the third day He rose again from the dead." Jesus' descent into hell is one of the more poorly understood Catholic beliefs. The First Letter of Peter tells us that after his death, Jesus preached to the spirits in prison (cf. 1 Pet 3:19). According to the *Catechism*, "Jesus, like all men, experienced death and in his soul joined the others in the realm of the dead. But he descended there as Savior, proclaiming the Good News to the spirits imprisoned there."[24] Hell, as we think of it now, must be distinguished from the pre-resurrection understanding of Sheol, or the abode of the dead mentioned in the Old Testament. All the dead, whether evil or righteous, were in Sheol as they awaited the Redeemer. After his death and before his Resurrection, Jesus preached the Gospel to the dead, bringing the message of salvation to complete fulfillment. In doing so, Jesus opened the gates of heaven to the righteous: "Jesus did not descend into hell to deliver the damned, nor to destroy the hell of damnation, but to free the just who had gone before him."[25]

[22] Pew Research Center, "Views on the Afterlife".
[23] *CCC* 1035.
[24] *CCC* 632.
[25] *CCC* 633.

It is important to note that God does not condemn anyone to hell; people condemn themselves by the grave sins they have committed and their refusal to repent of them and to accept God's forgiveness: "To die in mortal sin without repenting and accepting God's merciful love means remaining separated from him forever by our own free choice. This state of definitive self-exclusion from communion with God and the blessed is called 'hell.'"[26]

It stands to reason that if heaven is eternal union with God, hell is eternal separation from him. Scripture uses a variety of images and metaphors to convince us of how terrible hell must be: it is a "lake of fire" (Rev 20:15); a place of burning coals, brimstone, and scorching wind (cf. Ps 11:6); a place of darkness where men will weep and gnash their teeth (cf. Mt 25:30). According to the Pew Center, those who believe in hell believe people in it will experience psychological and physical suffering, will become aware of the suffering they created in the world, and will be excluded from a relationship with God.[27] As with heaven, being in hell is beyond our understanding and description.

So, while the Church readily affirms its existence, it does not say who is in hell. Through the process of canonization, the Church officially proclaims that after their death, some people become saints; that is, their souls have gone to heaven. There is no official damnation of anyone, even the most notorious historical figures like Hitler. Judas has never been officially declared damned to hell by the Church.

With that in mind, do we know for sure if anyone is in hell? Given what Catholics believe about dying in the state of mortal sin, judgment after death, and the existence of hell, it stands to reason there are souls in hell. But as

[26] CCC 1033.
[27] Pew Research Center, "Views on the Afterlife".

Hans Urs von Balthasar asked: May we hope that all men are saved? Is it possible that even though hell exists, it could be "empty"? (With the understanding that hell is not so much a place as a state of being and that the fallen angels are eternally damned.) In his book *Dare We Hope "That All Men Are Saved"?* Balthasar appeals to Scripture to help make his case that the Church can and should hope and pray for the salvation of all: "'For the grace of God has appeared for the salvation of all men' (Tit 2:11), according to God's will 'to reconcile to himself, whether on earth or in heaven' (Col 1:20), since God has decided 'to unite all things in him'(Christ) as the head (Eph 1:10)."[28] He also quotes the Gospel of John: "What dominates for [John] is the ring of the universal words: 'And I, when I am lifted up from the earth, will draw all men to myself' (12:32)."[29] He proposes that "the Old Testament image of judgment . . . may well have become clearer (the Judge is the Savior of all) and that, as a result, hope outweighs fear."[30] While a deep dive into Balthasar's theology is beyond the scope of this chapter, it is important to understand that Balthasar is clearly *not* saying that we have certain knowledge that all people are saved; in fact, he insists that damnation is a real possibility for anyone. Rather, he is proposing that we are *permitted* to hope that all will be saved.

Balthasar's provocative question has caused some to accuse him of universalism, the idea that everyone goes to heaven. If this were the case, they ask, why bother to evangelize, to proclaim the *euangelion*, the good news of Jesus Christ? But as Bishop Robert Barron states in his foreword

[28] Hans Urs Von Balthasar, *Dare We Hope "That All Men Be Saved"?*, trans. David Kipp and Lothar Krauth, 2nd ed. (San Francisco: Ignatius Press, 2014), 25.

[29] Balthasar, *Dare We Hope*, 27.

[30] Balthasar, *Dare We Hope*, 30.

to *Dare We Hope*, "The ardent witness of deeply committed evangelists, teachers and missionaries might well be precisely the means by which God deigns to bring his people to eternal life."[31] God "desires all men to be saved and to come to the knowledge of the truth. For there is one God, and there is one mediator between God and men, the man Christ Jesus, who gave himself as a ransom for all" (1 Tim 2:4–5). Since God desires all men to be saved, dare we hope his desire is fulfilled?

[31] Balthasar, *Dare We Hope*, xiii.

13

Death and Suffering

My father, Bob, was the quintessential Irish Catholic: faithful, but not terribly demonstrative. He lived a virtuous life marked more by example than by word. Unbeknownst to me, he suffered from depression much of his adult life. My mom never said anything, and I was not intuitive enough to notice. In his sixties, he embarked upon the slow death march of dementia.

As with most patients with dementia, the early stages were not all that obvious, except to those close enough to notice the subtle telltale signs of decline. At age sixty-eight, Bob was diagnosed with esophageal cancer. Surgery was brutal, with a prolonged convalescence marked by a series of complications. The trauma of cancer and surgery was like pouring gasoline on a fire: the simmering flames of comingled depression and dementia burst into a fireball. His sleepless nights were dominated by ruminations about hell. He no longer left the house, the only exception being a visit to our home for dinner where he sat quietly at the head of the table, listening to the banter of our five sons. He went into a cognitive and emotional free fall punctuated by a series of hospitalizations in a psychiatric hospital. In a last-ditch effort, his psychiatrist recommended electroconvulsive therapy (ECT), a treatment he received twice. Despite all the advances in pharmacologic treatments for depression, some patients continue to spiral downward, and the application

of electrical current to the sick brain can pull some patients
out of this vortex. Such was not the case for Bob.

In spite of everyone's best attempts, the combination of
cancer, depression, and dementia reduced my father to a
catatonic state. For the last few weeks of his life, he was
confined to a hospital bed, minimally communicative, able
to take only a few sips of nourishment. As if on a dimmer
switch, his body and mind quickly began to fade. Some say
he looked gaunt. I say he looked skeletal. My mom kept a
round-the-clock vigil, and on the eve of his death, I joined
her. As we sat in silence gazing on Bob, my mom softly said,
"When I see Bob, I see Christ."

In the eyes of the world, the existence of suffering is the
trump card in arguments against the existence of God. But
as Catholics, we know that God exists and that suffering
indeed has a purpose. In his humanity, Jesus shared in our
suffering, and our suffering is a way to share in his divin-
ity. Absent a suffering savior, our afflictions are meaningless.
But we believe in a Messiah who "was wounded for our
transgressions . . . bruised for our iniquities; upon him was
the chastisement that made us whole, and with his stripes
we are healed" (Is 53:5).

Pope Saint John Paul II best articulated the nature of redemptive suffering in his apostolic letter *Salvifici doloris*. First
and foremost, he explains, suffering is universal. In our fallen
world, suffering occurs whenever we experience any kind
of evil. And since we, as human beings, are a composite of
body and spirit, we suffer in this double dimension, experiencing both moral and physical suffering. In the face of its
universal nature, the experience of suffering inevitably stirs
up within us the question: Why? Why do I suffer? Why
does suffering even exist in the first place?

Scripture helps with the answer, says the pope. The story

of Job is the story of a just man who suffers greatly. He loses his family and all his possessions. Why? Accusing Job of having committed some sin, his friends tell him that he is receiving his just desserts from God. But Job protests: he has done nothing wrong; he has no reason to suffer. He cries out to God, demanding a response. Does God provide him with the answer to the question why? Unfortunately for Job, and for us, God does not. Rather, "his suffering is the suffering of someone who is innocent and it must be accepted as a mystery, which the individual is unable to penetrate completely by his own intelligence."[1]

It would be thoroughly unsatisfying if the only response to the reason for suffering was "It's a mystery." There must be more to it. And there is: "In order to perceive the true answer to the "why" of suffering, we must look to the revelation of divine love, the ultimate source of the meaning of everything that exists. Love is also the richest source of the meaning of suffering. . . . Christ causes us to enter into the mystery and to discover the "why" of suffering, as far as we are capable of grasping the sublimity of divine love."[2] Suffering is conquered by the love of Jesus Christ. How so?

Every suffering person has the need to be heard and to understand that Christ knows what it means to feel alone, neglected, and tormented by the prospect of pain.

In the Cross of Christ are concentrated all the sickness and suffering of the world: all the *physical suffering*, of which the Cross . . . is the symbol; all the *psychological suffering*, expressed in the death of Jesus in the darkest of solitude, abandonment and betrayal; all the *moral suffering*, manifested in the condemnation to death of one who is innocent; all the

[1] John Paul II, apostolic letter *Salvifici doloris* (On the Christian Meaning of Human Suffering) (February 11, 1984), no. 11.

[2] John Paul II, *Salvifici doloris*, no. 13.

spiritual suffering, displayed in a desolation that seems like the silence of God.[3]

Eternal life is only possible because of the salvific love of Christ: "For God so loved the world that he gave his only-begotten Son, that whoever believes in him should not perish but have eternal life" (Jn 3:16). Christ conquered sin and death on the cross. He gives us a way back to the Father. Even though his victory over sin and death does not abolish our suffering here on earth, it nevertheless throws a new light upon suffering: the light of salvation.[4]

As we endure the trials and tribulations of life, it is easy to lose sight of the definitive suffering: the loss of eternal life. As bad as things can be here on earth, this suffering pales in comparison to the suffering of damnation. Pain can overwhelm and shrink us so that we are unable to look beyond it and lose sight of what awaits us. Saint Paul encourages us to avoid this temptation: "I consider that the sufferings of this present time are not worth comparing with the glory that is to be revealed to us" (Rom 8:18).

So then, the salvific love of Christ sheds light upon the nature of suffering. But why did Christ have to suffer? Could not his love be shown in some other way? Was it really necessary for him to die on the cross? In short—yes. Yes, it was necessary for Jesus to suffer. Why? Pope John Paul II responds emphatically:

Christ goes towards his Passion and death with full awareness of the mission that he has to fulfil precisely in this way. Precisely by *means of this suffering* he must bring it about "that man should not perish, but have eternal life". Pre-

[3] Congregation of the Doctrine for the Faith, letter on the care of persons in the critical and terminal phases of life *Samaritanus bonus* (June 25, 2020), no. 2.

[4] *Salvifici doloris*, no. 15.

cisely by means of his Cross he must strike at the roots of evil, planted in the history of man and in human souls. Precisely by means of his Cross he must accomplish *the work of salvation*. This work, in the plan of eternal Love, has a redemptive character.[5]

It matters that Jesus suffers. It also matters how he suffers. Scripture had to be fulfilled. The prophet Isaiah tells of a messiah who will be "despised", "wounded for our transgressions", "bruised for our iniquities" (Is 53:3, 5). An innocent Messiah who suffers voluntarily. A Messiah who takes upon himself the sins of the entire world. "In his suffering, sins are cancelled out precisely because he alone as the only-begotten Son could take them upon himself, accept them *with that love for the Father which overcomes* the evil of every sin."[6] Christ gives the answer to the question of suffering through his own suffering.

But Jesus does not stop there. He suffered for us, but he wants us to participate with him through our sufferings. He wants us to share in his sufferings. Through Baptism, we become the adopted sons and daughters of God and heirs to his kingdom:

> For all who are led by the Spirit of God are sons of God. For you did not receive the spirit of slavery to fall back into fear, but you have received a spirit of sonship. When we cry, "Abba! Father!" it is the Spirit himself bearing witness with our spirit that we are children of God, and if children, then heirs, heirs of God and fellow heirs with Christ, provided we suffer with him in order that we may also be glorified with him. (Rom 8:14–17)

This is one of those "good news, not-so-good news" passages. Good news: we are children of God and heirs of God

[5] *Salvifici doloris*, no. 16.
[6] *Salvifici doloris*, no. 17.

and joint heirs with Christ. Not-so-good news: provided we suffer with him. If we are going to be glorified with him, we must suffer with him. This is the core of redemptive suffering.

As Saint John Paul II says, "Every man has *his own share in the Redemption*. Each one is also *called to share in that suffering* through which the Redemption was accomplished. . . . In bringing about the Redemption through suffering, Christ *has* also *raised human suffering to the level of Redemption*."[7]

Saint Paul goes even further: "Now I rejoice in my sufferings for your sake, and in my flesh I complete what is lacking in Christ's afflictions for the sake of his body, that is, the Church" (Col 1:24). Two things stand out: (1) Paul is rejoicing in his sufferings and (2) his sufferings matter because he is uniting them with the sufferings of Christ. In a strict sense, nothing is lacking in Christ's afflictions. His sacrifice was total and perfect, lacking in nothing. So, when Paul says his sufferings are completing what is lacking in Christ's afflictions, is he implying that the Redemption of Christ is somehow incomplete? No! What Paul means is that we are invited to participate in the redemptive suffering of Christ for the salvation of the world. "Yes, it seems to be part *of the very essence of Christ's redemptive suffering* that this suffering requires to be unceasingly completed."[8]

So, as we saw in Romans, we are joint heirs with Christ, which then makes us co-redeemers. And because we are co-redeemers, our sufferings, just like his, are offered for the sake of the Body of Christ, the Church. If suffering is taken in this context, it becomes possible to rejoice in it. Suffering matters.

---

[7] *Salvifici doloris*, no. 19.
[8] *Salvifici doloris*, no. 24.

So, how does all this play out in the real world? There will always be a mystical element of redemptive suffering that we do not fully understand. Even if I accept that my suffering matters, I may not ever fully understand *how* it matters. In our earthly lives, we may never see the good that arises from our suffering, even if we are intentional in uniting our trials with the Cross. It is a matter of faith. However, on occasion, the redemptive nature of suffering bears fruit that is tangible and experienced by others.

Redemptive suffering draws us into the heart of Jesus. Even in his comatose state, Bob's suffering pulled my mom into the mystery of the Cross. To see suffering in the light of the suffering Savior brings meaning to what appears to be meaningless. A lifetime of faithfulness prepared my dad for the day when he would die well, even when he could no longer participate in the preparation for his death.

The art of dying well does begin with the art of living well, but living well does not by any means guarantee that death will be easy. In fact, for many, if not most people, dying is anything but easy. It involves pain and suffering and loneliness. But as coheirs with Jesus, we are called to share in his suffering that we may also be glorified with him. As co-redeemers with Christ, we can rejoice in our sufferings as we offer them for the sake of his Body, the Church. "When I see Bob, I see Christ."

14

Anointing of the Sick

John was a relatively healthy, active sixty-five-year-old man. He had a long history of hypertension, and despite his and his doctor's best efforts, his blood pressure tended to run a bit on the high side. On what was an otherwise ordinary day, John was doing some yard work. He instantly dropped to his knees from the sudden onset of excruciating pain in the back of his head, as if coldcocked with a baseball bat. Remaining conscious, he staggered to his feet and stumbled into the house. His wife, Kathy, recognized immediately that something was terribly wrong. An ambulance arrived within minutes and transported John to the nearby Catholic hospital.

Moments after arrival, he was whisked to the CT scanner and diagnosed with a large hemorrhage of his cerebellum. The pressure of the hematoma occluded the normal flow of spinal fluid and he was developing hydrocephalus: the normally slit-like fluid spaces of the brain had ballooned to three times their normal size. The combination of the hematoma and the accumulation of spinal fluid was rapidly increasing the pressure in John's brain, and death was imminent unless surgery was performed right away.

John remained conscious, but he was becoming progressively lethargic, a sign of impending herniation of the brain. He was taken to an operating room, where nearly a dozen people were working feverishly to prepare for his surgery. What appeared to be utter chaos was actually a well-rehearsed series of movements: an additional IV was placed in John's arm; surgical instruments were organized on a table draped with sterile blue drapes; medications were drawn into syringes. The anesthesiologist was at the head of the operating table, poised to render John unconscious for placement of a breathing tube into his lungs.

Into this beehive walked Fr. B., dressed in a bright yellow jumpsuit draped over his black clerics. Fr. B. had not had time to change into scrubs, so he had thrown on a set of disposable paper overalls, his Roman collar peeking through the neck opening. Fr. B.'s voice boomed out: "In the name of the Father and of the Son and of the Holy Spirit." The room came to a complete standstill as eleven of the twelve people in the room made the sign of the cross. John was conscious enough to recognize his beloved pastor, and the creases of anxiety on his face relaxed as Fr. B. touched his forehead with oil and said: "Through this holy anointing may the Lord in his love and mercy help you with the grace of the Holy Spirit. May the Lord who frees you from sin save you and raise you up." John closed his eyes and everyone continued their preparations.

John's story illustrates the urgency and primacy of the sacraments in his life. Fr. B. did not appear by some happenstance. He appeared in the operating room dressed in yellow paper overalls because the sacraments were the conduit of grace in John's life, and his family knew this. At the moment when John's life might be coming to an unanticipated, abrupt ending, their first priority was to call a priest. John is sick. He might be dying. Call a priest.

From ancient times, the Church has professed that the anointing of the sick is one of the seven sacraments instituted by Christ. "This sacrament gives the grace of the

Holy Spirit to those who are sick: by this grace the whole person is helped and saved, sustained by trust in God, and strengthened against the temptations of the Evil One and against anxiety over death."[1] The apostle James encouraged the faithful, "Is any among you sick? Let him call for the elders of the Church, and let them pray over him, anointing him with oil in the name of the Lord; and the prayer of faith will save the sick, and the Lord will raise them up; and if he has committed sins, he will be forgiven" (Jas 5:14–15).

Various councils (Florence, Trent, Vatican II) have produced documents that explain the theology and the norms associated with this sacrament. Historically known as "extreme unction", the Anointing of the Sick is administered not only to those near the point of death, but to any person who is seriously ill, undergoing surgery, or in a generally weakened condition. The sacrament can be repeated if the sick person recovers but later falls ill or if during the same illness becomes even more seriously ill. The Sacrament of the Anointing of the Sick should be given at the onset of a serious illness. As death draws near, the rite for Viaticum (literally "food for the journey") is the last sacrament of Christian life. (The rite of Viaticum will be covered in more detail later.)

The only proper minister for the Anointing of the Sick is a priest. The sacrament can take place within the Mass, although most often it is given outside the Mass. It can be celebrated at the church, the hospital, or the sick person's home, and the norms for the sacrament vary somewhat

[1] International Commission on English in the Liturgy, *Pastoral Care of the Sick: Rites of Anointing and Viaticum* (Totowa, N.J.: Catholic Book Publishing Co., 1983), para. 6, p. 21, as approved by the National Conference of Catholic Bishops and confirmed by the Apostolic See. Much of the information in this section can be found in this book.

depending on location. While by no means limited to the end of life, the Sacrament of Reconciliation is particularly important in the final preparation for death. If the sick person desires to confess, this should occur before the anointing.

The anointing of the sick includes introductory rites —a sprinkling with holy water and the penitential rite— followed by the Liturgy of the Word. The Liturgy of Anointing is next, and it has three distinct parts: the prayer of faith, the laying on of hands, and the anointing with oils. The laying on of hands is important for a number of reasons. It is a sign of blessing and an invocation for the Holy Spirit to come upon the sick person. Most important, the laying on of hands recalls the ministry of Jesus, who healed by the touch of his hands (see Lk 4:40, Mk 10:16).

All sacraments have a proper form—the words and actions performed—and a proper matter—the materials used. For the Anointing of the Sick, the proper matter is oil that has been blessed by the bishop, usually during Holy Week. Over the centuries, oil has been used to soothe and comfort the sick and weary, so the anointing with oil gives strength against the spiritual and physical threats of illness. The sick person is anointed on the forehead and on the hands, which signifies healing, strengthening, and the presence of the Holy Spirit. A generous use of oil is encouraged so that it is experienced as a sign of the Holy Spirit's healing power, and the oil is not wiped away for the same reason.

While the Anointing of the Sick is celebrated at the beginning of a serious illness, Viaticum is Holy Communion given when a person is near death. Viaticum is known as food for the passage from life to death and is the sacrament proper to the dying Catholic: "It is the completion and crown of the Christian life on this earth, signifying that the Christian follows the Lord to eternal glory and the banquet of the heavenly kingdom."[2] The importance of Viaticum cannot be overstated; ministers entrusted with the spiritual care of the sick should do everything possible to bring the Eucharist to someone in danger of death. Unique to the celebration of Viaticum is the renewal of the baptismal profession of faith, which is a renewal and a fulfillment of initiation into the Church. If the person who has received the Eucharist as Viaticum lingers, it is proper to celebrate Viaticum as often as possible, even daily, until death occurs. If possible, it is preferable to receive Communion under both species of bread and wine.

You might ask, "What ever happened to John?" As it turned out, John not only survived but made a full recovery. After leaving the hospital, he spent some time in a rehabilitation facility. I saw him about a month after his surgery, and I asked him if he remembered the events I described above. Not surprisingly, he could not recall many details of that particular day, just fleeting images and sounds. When I asked him if he remembered seeing Fr. B. in the operating room, he responded only with a warm smile and a nod of the head. That's the beauty of the grace of any sacrament —you might not remember the details (I certainly don't remember my own baptism!), yet there is an awareness of the mystery received.

---

[2] International Commission on English in the Liturgy, *Pastoral Care of the Sick*, 158.

15

Food for the Journey

The third of twelve children, Ramon was born in central Mexico. He immigrated to the United States with his wife, Maria, in 1983, and they have five grown children. Like many Mexican immigrants to the United States, Ramon found employment in a meatpacking plant. Ramon is soft spoken, yet confident and intelligent. Under different circumstances, he might have become a highly educated professional. Even so, it is not *what he does* that distinguishes him; it is *who he is* in Christ. Ramon integrates love of God and love of neighbor seamlessly. He is a pillar in his parish, serving as a lector and an extraordinary minister of Holy Communion. He is a longtime member of the Christian Family Movement and a recently ordained permanent deacon.

As the COVID-19 pandemic raged in Mexico, Ramon received notice that his mother had contracted the virus and was not doing well. Ramon had just recovered from his own COVID infection a few weeks earlier. Knowing that his recent illness afforded him some degree of immunity, he and his wife traveled to his hometown in Mexico to be with his mother, who continued to decline.

At seventy-one years old, his mother was relatively young but was beset by a number of medical conditions that made her vulnerable to the effects of the virus. The hospital closest to his town was overwhelmed by the surge. Supplies were scarce, and the outlook was grim for anyone with a severe infection. Knowing that she could not receive visitors once hospitalized and knowing that the hospital had little to offer, Ramon's mother elected to remain at home, sequestered in a bedroom with her husband, who was engaged in his own battle against the virus. Ramon's siblings kept vigil in the adjacent living room, trying their best to protect themselves from infection yet ministering to their mother and father without the benefit of protective equipment.

Ramon's journey home was an exercise in frustration, as mechanical breakdowns and scheduling delays extended his airline travel an additional twelve hours. His late arrival prevented him from immediately heading to his hometown; no taxi drivers were willing to take the risk of traveling at night through towns and neighborhoods plagued by the violence of drug cartels.

The next morning, he set off for his village, and as he approached, he received a frantic call from his sister, who pleaded with him to hurry as their mother slipped further and further into diminished levels of consciousness. Upon his arrival, his mother briefly rallied and was more alert, raising hopes for a miraculous recovery. Ramon seated himself at the bedside of his mother and father and led the Rosary, intoning the beginning of each prayer, which his siblings completed from the adjoining room.

Ramon's immediate next desire was to bring the Eucharist to his dying mother. However, this proved to be a more arduous task than he had anticipated. The COVID pandemic sowed seeds of fear, and fear can lead some people to make irrational decisions. The parish in Ramon's village was led by a priest who lived elsewhere, but who would travel to say Mass and administer the sacraments. For reasons that are difficult to understand, this priest refused to allow anyone to bring Eucharist to a COVID patient. While it may be understandable that the priest would not put himself in harm's way, his unwillingness to let others bring Jesus to the sick made little sense.

By now, it was Sunday. Undaunted, Ramon widened his search for Holy Communion. He felt it was imperative that he bring Viaticum, food for the journey, to his dying mother. He called the pastor of the next closest parish, some fifteen miles away. This priest was about to begin Mass and initially refused to allow Ramon to bring the Eucharist to his mother. However, after saying Mass, the priest had a change of heart and acquiesced to Ramon's request, allowing it for this one instance since Ramon was in formation to become a deacon.

When Ramon arrived, the priest kept his distance but deposited a few Hosts in the pyx Ramon had brought. The drive back home was a solemn, reverent procession; no music on the radio, no talking. The silence was broken only by a brief phone call to the siblings, telling them to prepare an altar in the front room in anticipation of the arrival of the Body of Christ. In Ramon's words, "They prepared everything as beautiful as possible, not as Jesus deserves, but the best we could offer."

In the presence of the Eucharist, Ramon's mother was invigorated and joined with the rest of the family as they sang a hymn, made an Act of Contrition, and said the Lord's Prayer. In unison they prayed, "Lord, I am not worthy that you should enter under my roof, but only say the word and my soul shall be healed."

Ramon gave his mother Viaticum, and she was even stronger for a little bit and was able to join the family in singing some of their favorite hymns. She thanked everyone and encouraged them to lead a good life, living in fraternity with each other. Within minutes, her strength faded, and she became unresponsive as she continued her silent journey toward death. She died the following morning, a Monday.

During the pandemic, local regulations required burial of a deceased COVID patient within five hours of death, regardless of the time of day, which led to some burials in the middle of the night. Failure to comply with this rule resulted in government officials confiscating and cremating the body. The responsibility for grave preparation fell to family members, and so as soon as Ramon's mother died, extended family and friends gathered under the rising sun at the cemetery to dig her grave. Meanwhile, a representative from the local undertaker arrived at the family house with a coffin. However, he would not touch the body. Ramon, along with a brother, placed his mother's body into a zippered bag, which was then secured in the coffin in the front room of the house.

It took four hours to dig the grave by hand. In the meantime, Ramon and his siblings kept vigil over their mother's remains as Ramon led them in prayer. A priest was not available; no funeral Mass was offered. Once the grave was finally ready, the family accompanied the coffin to the cemetery. Ramon's father, still sick with COVID, remained at home, unable to attend the burial of his wife. At the cemetery, the family, led by Ramon, once again prayed the Rosary. The coffin was then lowered into the ground while shovelfuls of dirt rained down.

As he told this story, Ramon's grief was still raw. All these events had occurred in just the prior week. However, bringing his mother Viaticum was an enormous consolation. He recalled her eagerness to receive the Eucharist and the happiness she experienced. Just prior to receiving Holy Communion, she was anxious, straining to breathe, trying to sit up in bed. She was unable to swallow, so Ramon gave her a tiny piece of the Host, knowing it would dissolve under her tongue. Immediately, she became calm and smiled. In Ramon's words, "It was like giving water to the thirsty or food to the hungry. She was happy, she was loved, and she took Jesus for the way, for the journey."

Viaticum—food for the journey. It is the reception of the Eucharist as death approaches. It is the completion and crown of the Christian life on earth. It is the hope for the resurrection, for Jesus said, "He who eats my flesh and drinks my blood has eternal life, and I will raise him up at the last day" (Jn 6:54).

> Viaticum is the Holy Eucharist received by those who are about to leave this earthly life and are preparing for the journey to eternal life. Communion in the body and blood of Christ who died and rose from the dead, received at the moment of passing from this world to the Father, is the seed of eternal life and the power of the resurrection.[1]

The word *Viaticum* is taken from the ancient Greek custom of sharing a meal with those about to set out on a journey. The early Church recognized the importance of this particular reception of the Eucharist. As early as A.D. 325 at the Council of Nicaea, the Holy Eucharist given to the dying was called the "last and most necessary Viaticum".[2]

The Sacrament of the Anointing of the Sick should be celebrated at the beginning of a serious illness, while Viaticum is meant to be received when death is close.[3] Whenever possible, Viaticum should be celebrated within the Mass.

---

[1] United States Conference of Catholic Bishops, *Compendium: Catechism of the Catholic Church* (Washington, D.C.: USCCB Publishing, 2006), no. 320.

[2] Catholic Encyclopedia, s.v. "Viaticum", New Advent, newadvent.org/cathen/15397c.htm, accessed February 2, 2021.

[3] The norms for Viaticum are taken from International Commission on

However, more often, Viaticum is received in the home, in the hospital, or in another facility where the person is dying. Family members and friends should be invited to participate in the planning and celebration. If at all possible, Viaticum is celebrated while the dying person is able to take part and respond.

The baptismal profession of faith by the dying person is an important part of the celebration; it is a renewal of his initial commitment to the Christian faith and a fulfillment of the initiation into the Christian mysteries, Baptism leading to the Eucharist. Whether celebrated within or outside of Mass, the Sign of Peace is included in the rite. This gives those present the opportunity to embrace the dying Christian, recognizing he will be gone soon, yet expressing the joy of Christian hope in the resurrection. Communion can be given as the Precious Blood, the Precious Body, or both. If celebrated outside the Mass, the Precious Blood must be transported in a vessel that eliminates the possibility of spilling.

If the person receiving Viaticum continues to live, he can continue to receive the Eucharist as Viaticum frequently, even daily, until death. The rite can be simplified as needed depending on the condition of the dying person. The ordinary ministers of Viaticum are a priest or a deacon. However, if no ordained minister is available, any member of the faithful who has been duly appointed may give Viaticum.

Preceded by the Sacraments of Reconciliation and the Anointing of the Sick, Viaticum is the final waystation on

English in the Liturgy, *Pastoral Care of the Sick: Rites of Anointing and Viaticum* (Totowa, N.J.: Catholic Book Publishing Co., 1983), as approved by the National Conference of Catholic Bishops and confirmed by the Apostolic See.

the journey from life into death. In the *Catechism of the Catholic Church*, we read:

> The Christian who unites his own death to that of Jesus views it as a step towards him and an entrance into everlasting life. When the Church for the last time speaks Christ's words of pardon and absolution over the dying Christian, seals him for the last time with a strengthening anointing, and gives him Christ in viaticum as nourishment for the journey, she speaks with gentle assurance.

> Go forth, Christian soul, from this world
> in the name of God the almighty Father,
> who created you,
> in the name of Jesus Christ, the Son of the living God,
> who suffered for you,
> in the name of the Holy Spirit,
> who was poured out upon you.
> Go forth, faithful Christian!
> May you live in peace this day,
> may your home be with God in Zion,
> with Mary, the virgin Mother of God,
> with Joseph, and all the angels and saints. . . .
> May you return to [your Creator]
> who formed you from the dust of the earth.
> May holy Mary, the angels, and all the saints
> come to meet you as you go forth from this life. . . .
> May you see your Redeemer face to face.[4]

---

[4] *CCC* 1020, quoting International Commission on English in the Liturgy, *Order of Christian Funerals*, Prayer of Commendation.

16

Funerals and Wakes

My earliest memories of Catholic funerals are from about the fourth grade, when I volunteered as an altar server at funeral Masses. My initial motivations were not terribly devout; it was an opportunity to skip class, ride in a fancy car to the cemetery, and eat funeral potatoes. Despite those less-than-pure reasons, the Mass had an impact on me. I was drawn in by the Scriptures proclaiming the hope of the resurrection, the smoke and the aroma of incense, the somber placing of the pall, the sprinkling of the graveside, and so on. There was and still is a powerful mystery present at the funeral liturgy that is imprinted on my heart to this day. While it is not officially known as the Mass of the Resurrection, that is how I think of a Catholic funeral Mass, one that recalls Christ's Resurrection from the dead and the anticipation of our own resurrection from the dead when he returns in glory.

A few funeral Masses are in the forefront of my memory. As an altar boy, I watched a devastated father, overcome with grief, as he single-handedly carried a miniature casket bearing his deceased newborn. I was the lector at the funeral of a high school friend, and the presiding priest, his uncle, gifted me with my friend's Bible. I walked into the cathedral behind my father-in-law's casket as the entire congregation was on their feet, hands upraised, loudly proclaiming in song, "How Great Thou Art". The church was packed, and the altar was lined with priests who came to celebrate the funeral of a simple telephone repairman. I preached at the funeral of my mother-in-law with the bishop of Grand Island presiding and dozens of grandchildren and great-grandchildren sitting in the pews. For months, her children had prepared for this day, each reading, each song carefully chosen in advance. Inspired by the Holy Spirit, my wife, Sharon, became choirmaster at the graveside, leading everyone in singing (in the round!) Mary Ann's favorite song, "Rejoice in the Lord Always". Who sings at the graveside?

My own father's funeral and graveside service mirrored his final years: difficult yet surprisingly joyful. Like a locomotive gathering steam, his dementia started slowly, but then gradually accelerated, reaching peak speed and then coming to a crashing halt at his death. Dementia was comingled with depression and cancer, and his final years were a strain on my mother, Judy. It should come as no surprise that his wake, funeral, and graveside service reflected both the difficulty and joy of these years.

Just as my father did not gently pass from this world to the next, the winter of 2007 did not gently dissolve into spring. My father died on Tuesday, February 27, and the wake was scheduled for Friday with the funeral to follow on Saturday. Just when you would think the ground would begin to thaw and no more than a dusting of snow would be expected, a late winter blizzard unloaded a foot of snow and ice on eastern Nebraska, closing schools, businesses, and major highways. Family members attempting to attend services were stranded in central Iowa. Only those with four-wheel drive were able to make their way to the wake service at the funeral home, and attendance was sparse. His septuagenarian and octogenarian friends stayed home.

Michael, my oldest son and the oldest Doran grandchild, spoke eloquently about his grandfather. They had the same birthday. To this day, a friend of mine remembers nothing of the wake other than the high school senior's words. The next day, the snow stopped, but the roads were still mostly impassable. The sun was blindingly bright as it reflected off the twelve inches of snow that had drifted into mounds double or triple that height from the gale force winds. The brilliant sun lifted our spirits, but the howling wind lowered our heads as we made our way into the church.

Much to my surprise, not only was his beloved pastor present to preside over the Mass, several other priests had made their way to concelebrate, including representatives from the Jesuit high school our boys attended. Providentially, a college classmate of mine happened to be in town; she also happened to be a professional mezzo-soprano and was in rehearsal for an opera premiere. Even though I had not seen her in decades, she graciously agreed to interrupt her schedule to sing at my father's funeral. The power of her voice filled the church as she sang a favorite of my mom's: "How Can I Keep from Singing?"

> Through all the tumult and the strife,
> I hear that music ringing;
> It finds an echo in my soul—
> How can I keep from singing?[1]

It was a beautiful metaphor for my dad's life and his funeral, but even more so for his graveside service. The sky was devoid of a single cloud, but the wind continued to howl, with gusts well above forty miles per hour. The winding

[1] Robert Lowry, *Bright Jewels for the Sunday School* (New York: Biglow & Main, 1809), 16.

road through the cemetery had been plowed first thing that morning, but quickly drifted over from the winds. Grandchildren carried the casket through the snow to the open grave. A two-sided tent had been erected to ward off the wind, but it was only minimally effective. The clamor of the wind-whipped canvas against the aluminum rods only further heightened the sense of urgency to bring the service to a quick end.

Despite the brevity of the service, conditions had deteriorated even further, and any vehicle without four-wheel drive was stuck. My uncle from Chicago had arrived ahead of the storm and had rented a Chevy PT Cruiser, the most non-snow-worthy car imaginable. Leather-soled Sunday-best shoes provided no traction as the priest, the pall bearers, and the hearse driver teamed up to extract the car and push it up the icy pathway out of the cemetery. No doubt my dad would have enjoyed the spectacle. I still laugh as I think about it.

The common thread among all these funerals was the Mass: in each case, the hope of the resurrection was proclaimed through the prayers, Scripture passages, and homily. As it says in the General Introduction to the Order of Christian Funerals:

> In the face of death, the Church confidently proclaims that God has created each person for eternal life and that Jesus, the Son of God, by his Death and Resurrection, has broken the chains of sin and death that bound human dignity. . . . At the death of a Christian, whose life of faith was begun in the waters of Baptism and strengthened at the Eucharistic table, the Church intercedes on behalf of the deceased because of its confident belief that death is not the end nor does it break the bonds forged in life. . . . The celebration

of the Christian funeral brings hope and consolation to the living.[2]

Vigil for the Deceased

The Catholic funeral rite is divided into several parts, each with its own purpose. The vigil service, also known as the wake, usually takes place during a time of visitation and viewing at a funeral home. However, the vigil can also take place in the church the evening before the funeral Mass or even in the home of the deceased. A growing recent trend is to forgo the vigil service and have a period of visitation and viewing just prior to the funeral. While this reduces the amount of time commitment (and presumably stress) for the family and friends of the deceased, having the visitation just prior to the funeral bypasses an important part of the funeral rites. "At the vigil, the Christian community keeps watch with the family in prayer to the God of mercy and finds strength in Christ's presence. It is the first occasion among the funeral rites for the solemn reading of the Word of God."[3] The vigil is also the time for family and friends to remember the life of the deceased, and for this reason, eulogies are most properly done during the vigil service.

As mentioned in the *Order of Christian Funerals*, "The time following death is often one of bewilderment and may involve shock or heartrending grief for the family and close friends . . . the experience of death can bring about in the mourners possible needs for reconciliation."[4] When confronted with the reality of death, it is natural for people to

[2] International Commission on English in the Liturgy, *Order of Christian Funerals* (Totowa, N.J.: Catholic Book Publishing Co., 2019), 2.

[3] ICEL, *Order of Christian Funerals*, para. 56, p. 23.

[4] ICEL, *Order of Christian Funerals*, paras. 52–53, p. 21.

contemplate their own mortality, which may bring to mind past sins and failings, and the Sacrament of Reconciliation brings much-needed healing of the soul during this time of grieving.

The basic parts of the vigil are the introductory rites, Liturgy of the Word, prayer of intercession, and concluding rite. The Liturgy of the Word includes reading from either the Old or New Testament, a responsorial psalm and a Gospel reading. A wide range of Bible passages is available, and while a number of themes can be found in these readings, the overarching message is the mercy of God and the hope for the resurrection of the dead. If the vigil takes place at a location outside the church, there is a specific rite for family and friends as they prepare to accompany the body of the deceased in the procession to the church or place of committal. The transfer of the body may be an especially emotional event, as this is the time of initial separation of the mourners from the deceased. The Rite of Transfer of the Body to the Church or to the Place of Committal recognizes this and offers prayers that remind those present of the solace of God's love. The rite concludes with Psalm 122, a song of encouragement to family and friends, "I rejoiced because they said to me, 'We will go to the house of the Lord.'"[5]

The Funeral Liturgy

What is perhaps most striking about a Christian funeral is its tone. While recognizing that death brings a profound sense of loss to those left behind, the funeral Mass is full of hope and joy. At the funeral liturgy, the "community

---

[5] Ps 122:1, as quoted in ICEL, *Order of Christian Funerals*, para. 127, p. 72.

gathers with the family and friends of the deceased to give praise and thanks to God for Christ's victory over sin and death, to commend the deceased to God's tender mercy and compassion, and to seek strength in the proclamation of the Paschal Mystery."[6] The funeral liturgy has four main parts: Reception at the Church, Liturgy of the Word, Liturgy of the Eucharist, and Final Commendation and Farewell.

The Church is the place where Christian life begins in Baptism and is nourished by the Eucharist, and where the community gathers to commend the deceased person to the Lord's care. For this reason, the Rite of Reception is especially important, because, "In the act of receiving the body, the members of the community acknowledge the deceased as one of their own, as one who was welcomed in Baptism and who held a place in the assembly."[7] In a sense, the Reception at the Church is the final homecoming. The rite typically begins at the entrance of the church and marks the beginning of the funeral liturgy. Any national flags or other insignia are removed at this time, and the funeral pall is placed over the casket, often by family and friends. The paschal candle can be used during this occasion.

During the Liturgy of the Word, one or two readings are read prior to the Gospel reading. Family members are encouraged to choose the readings and music for the funeral Mass. Normally, the readings from the vigil service are not repeated during the funeral liturgy.

The readings proclaim the Paschal Mystery, teach remembrance of the dead, convey the hope of being gathered together again in God's Kingdom, and encourage the witness

[6] ICEL, *Order of Christian Funerals*, para. 129, p. 72.
[7] ICEL, *Order of Christian Funerals*, para. 131, p. 72.

of Christian life. Above all, the readings tell of God's design for a world in which suffering and death will relinquish their hold on all whom God has called his own.[8]

If possible, the Responsorial Psalm is sung as the community expresses its grief and praise. A brief homily follows the Liturgy of the Word, but never any kind of eulogy. After the homily, the Liturgy of the Eucharist is celebrated in the usual fashion. Members of the family or friends of the deceased should bring the gifts to the altar. The singing of the parts of the Mass is again encouraged. The altar and gifts can be incensed by the priest, and the deacon may incense the priest and congregation.

Following the Prayer after Communion, the Final Commendation and Farewell takes place.

The final commendation is a final farewell by the members of the community, an act of respect for one of their members, whom they entrust to the tender and merciful embrace of God. This act of last farewell also acknowledges the reality of separation and affirms that the community and the deceased, baptized into the one Body, share the same destiny, resurrection on the last day.[9]

The body is sprinkled with holy water, which is a reminder that Baptism marks the person for eternal life. The body is also incensed, which signifies respect for the body as a temple of the Holy Spirit. If possible, the song of farewell is actually sung. The song of farewell affirms hope and trust in the Paschal Mystery. At its completion, a procession is formed to accompany the body to the place of committal.

[8] ICEL, *Order of Christian Funerals*, para. 137, p. 73.
[9] ICEL, *Order of Christian Funerals*, para. 146, p. 75.

Rite of Committal

The Rite of Committal marks the conclusion of the funeral rites.

> In committing the body to its resting place, the community expresses the hope that, with all those who have gone before marked with the sign of faith, the deceased awaits the glory of the resurrection. The rite of committal is an expression of the communion that exists between the Church on earth and the Church in heaven: the deceased passes with the farewell prayers of the community of believers into the welcoming company of those who need faith no longer but see God face to face.[10]

At times, a final commendation does not take place during the funeral liturgy or there is not a funeral that precedes the committal. In these cases, the Final Commendation occurs during the Rite of Committal.

Through the act of committal, "the community of faith proclaims that the grave or place of interment, once a sign of futility and despair, has been transformed by means of Christ's own Death and Resurrection into a sign of hope and promise."[11] The Rite of Committal includes Scripture and a prayer over the place of committal. The prayer over the place of committal varies depending on whether the grave or tomb has already been blessed or if the final deposition of the body will actually take place at a later time (such as when the body is to be cremated or when weather delays burial).

The funeral rites for children have a few adaptations that reflect that "the Christian community is challenged in a

[10] ICEL, *Order of Christian Funerals*, para. 206, p. 110.
[11] ICEL, *Order of Christian Funerals*, para. 209, p. 110.

particular way by the death of an infant of child. The bewilderment and pain that death causes can be overwhelming in this situation, especially for the parents and brothers and sisters of the deceased child."[12] As other children are likely to be present, the prayers and Scripture passages should be chosen with them in mind. The rite is slightly different for children whose parents intended them to be baptized but who died before Baptism.

The COVID-19 pandemic was disruptive to daily life in a great many ways, and funerals were no exception. At times during the pandemic, gatherings at churches were frequently prohibited completely or the number of those allowed to be present was severely restricted. Because of this, many funerals were conducted with a minimal number of family or friends present, and in many situations, the funerals were delayed for months until COVID restrictions had passed. Insult was added to injury and the process of mourning painfully prolonged.

---

[12] ICEL, *Order of Christian Funerals*, para. 238, p. 132.

17

Cremation

Jed is a scrub tech. He hands instruments to me as I perform an operation. He is good at his job and is quite funny. He is known for his impressions of surgeons, although he claims that he has never done one of me (I'm skeptical). Jed is also a faithful Christian. He attends church regularly and occasionally his quips have a Scripture passage hidden within.

Fortunately, most surgeries are relatively routine and the atmosphere relaxed. One day, during a particularly long surgery, Jed told the story of his good friend Joe.

Joe was many things to many people: a husband, a father, a coach to his daughter's soccer team, and an avid outdoorsman. Jed had many fond memories of duck hunting with Joe and a cadre of like-minded friends. Joe unfortunately passed away in an auto accident; it was an instant, powerful loss to the close group of hunting friends.

His funeral was filled with guests clad in red, as he was a huge fan of the Nebraska Cornhuskers football team. The entire hunting group sat up front together, and each one of the pallbearers was someone from the hunting posse. The ensuing celebration of life that took place afterward was filled with waterfowl, big game, and fishing stories that were a mixed bag of deep belly laughs and stifled sniffles emanating from a bunch of redneck hunters trying not to cry in front of one another.

Joe was cremated shortly afterward, and his wife gave some of his ashes to the friend who had known him the longest. Fast forward a few months to mid-October of that year, when the group took a pilgrimage to Valentine, Nebraska, for their yearly duck hunting trip. As dawn approached, they all headed out in two separate boats to their favorite spot. As they were waiting for first light to break over the horizon, the friend who was given Joe's ashes poured some of them into the end of his barrel and then passed the rest to the next man, who did the same. The remains were passed on from man to man until each of them had some of Joe's ashes in his shotgun. As Jed remembered,

> We were sitting in that boat with those close friends, all waiting to fire at the first wave of ducks. A quiet calm came over our atmosphere with none of us breaking the silence that held sway over our gathering. We all felt like we were getting our own chance to honor our friend in our own unique way. And just like it was meant to be, a group of ducks flew into our decoy spread. We all stood up and fired our guns. I cannot remember for the life of me if any of us hit anything, but I can recall in crystal clarity that in that foggy early light, we all rose together and celebrated our friend's memory in a fitting way.

As Jed talked, the rest of the crew in the operating room listened intently, alternating between reverent silence and bursts of laughter. The story was somber yet incredibly funny. With Jed's gift for gab, he painted an image of a bunch of rubes launching volley after volley of the carbon remains of Joe from the barrel of a twelve-gauge. Those who weren't constrained by their sterile gowns dabbed the corners of their eyes as tears of laughter commingled with sadness trickled down their cheeks.

While Jed thought the story was fittingly humorous, he did not think it was disrespectful. After all, they were honoring a beloved friend who would have thoroughly enjoyed the celebration. Where was the harm? In fact, from the perspective of Jed and his friends, they were doing the right thing, because that is what Joe would have wanted.

No doubt, we have all heard similar stories of cremated remains being stored on a book shelf, placed inside a locket that is worn around the neck, or scattered over a piece of ground or body of water that was particularly important to the deceased. The final resting place of Joe was no different, although admittedly his mode of transportation was a bit more dramatic.

Some may argue that keeping ashes of the deceased on the mantel or in a locket is a sign of respect and a way of remembering. It seems better than the desires of the ancient Greek philosopher Diogenes, who wanted his dead body thrown over the city walls to be eaten by wild beasts. After all, the body is useless after death and worth nothing, right?

The story of Joe (and Diogenes) raises an important question: Does it matter what happens to the body after death? Do we have a duty to treat human remains in a particular way? The answer is yes, it does matter, and we do have the responsibility to treat the body of a deceased person in a fashion that is commensurate with his dignity as a person made in the image and likeness of God.

In keeping with this desire to maintain the dignity of the body, which will be subject to the resurrection of the dead, the Church has long expressed a preference for burial over cremation. (Recently, alkaline hydrolysis and body composting after death have gained popularity as methods of disposing

human remains.)[1] Scripture is replete with examples of burial as the primary way to treat a dead body: to bury his

[1] Alkaline hydrolysis is the chemical process of dissolving a body in a base
solution with heat and pressure, resulting in a mixture of solid bones and
teeth surrounded by a sterile fluid of amino acids, salts, and sugars. The fluid
is drained into the sewage and the solid remains then pulverized and placed
in an urn. Alkaline hydrolysis has been advocated by some as more envi-
ronmentally friendly than either burial (cemeteries require large amounts of
land that could be used for other purposes) or cremation (which adds carbon
emissions to the atmosphere). The Church has no official teaching on alkaline
hydrolysis, but a number of ethicists have weighed in on the subject. Some
have objected to alkaline hydrolysis, saying that "flushing remains down the
drain" is not consistent with respect for bodily dignity. However, cremation
involves sending human bodies "up in smoke" with ashes raining down on
the heads of anyone walking nearby. Objectively, there is probably little moral
distinction between the two methods. Alkaline hydrolysis is relatively new
in the United States, being legal in sixteen states as of 2020.
   Body composting is another way to treat the body after death, using the
bacteria already present in a body to cause decomposition. The body is
placed in a reusable vessel, covered with wood chips, and aerated, which
creates an environment for microbes and essential bacteria. The body, over
a span of about thirty days, is fully transformed into soil. After thirty days,
the vessel is opened, bone fragments are ground to small shards, and any
remaining nonorganic material is removed (for example, artificial joints
or other metal). Family members can then use the composted remains as
fertilizer. As of 2022, body composting is legal in five states. See Alex
Brown, "California Legalizes Human Composting", Pew (website of the
Pew Charitable Trusts), September 20, 2022, pewtrusts.org/en/research-and-
analysis/blogs/stateline/2022/09/20/california-legalizes-human-composting.
   The Committee on Doctrine of the United States Conference of Catholic
Bishops has voiced its disapproval of alkaline hydrolysis and body composting: "The guidance offered by the Congregation regarding burial and cremation reflects the Church's overarching concern that due respect be shown to
the bodily remains of the deceased in a way that gives visible witness to our
faith and hope in the resurrection of the body. Unfortunately, the two most
prominent newer methods for disposition of bodily remains that are proposed
as alternatives to burial and cremation, alkaline hydrolysis and human composting, fail to meet this criterion." Committee on Doctrine United States
Conference of Catholic Bishops, *On the Proper Disposal of Human Remains*,
March 20, 2023, no. 8.

wife, Sarah, Abraham paid full price for the cave at Mach-pelah (Gen 23:9); the Book of Tobit describes burial of the dead as an act of charity (1:17–18); Lazarus was buried in a tomb four days before being raised by Jesus (Jn 11:17); most importantly, the body of Jesus was laid in the tomb meant for Joseph of Arimathea (Mt 27:57–60). Traditional practices, such as veneration of saints at their tombs, demonstrate the Church's preference for burial. Burying the dead is one of the seven corporal acts of mercy. In the fourth century, Augustine wrote not only of the importance of burying the dead but also of where the dead should be buried:

> Yet it follows not that the bodies of the departed are to be despised and flung aside, and above all of just and faithful men, which bodies as organs and vessels to all good works their spirit has holily used. . . .
>
> Doubtless also the providing for the interment of bodies a place at the Memorials of Saints, is a mark of a good human affection toward the remains of one's friends: since if there be religion in the burying, there cannot but be religion in taking thought where the burying shall be.[2]

The Church did not find it necessary to express a preference for burial until the nineteenth century. Atheist French revolutionaries encouraged cremation, as a demonstration against the "shackles of religious superstition".[3] Secular materialist societies, such as the Freemasons, likewise encouraged cremation. At the end of the century, the Vatican responded with a prohibition against cremation and joining

[2] Augustine, *On Care to Be Had for the Dead*, in *A Select Library of the Nicene and Post-Nicene Fathers of the Christian Church*, ed. Philip Schaff, D.D., LL.D. (Buffalo, The Christian Literature Company, 1887), 3:541–42.

[3] Scott Hahn, *Hope to Die: The Christian Meaning of Death and the Resurrection of the Body* (Steubenville, Ohio: Emmaus Road Publishing, 2020), 130.

societies that promote cremation. A few years later, this prohibition was included in the 1917 Code of Canon Law, canon 1203: "The bodies of the faithful must be buried, and cremation is reprobated. If anyone has in any manner ordered his body to be cremated, it shall be unlawful to execute his wish; if this order has been attached to a contract, a last will, or any other document, it is to be considered as not added."[4] While the Church was forbidding cremation in its own right, she was also addressing the anti-Catholic organizations that encouraged cremation.

Over the following decades, the societal norms surrounding cremation gradually changed, and in 1963, Pope Paul VI lifted the ban on cremation, while maintaining the Church's preference for burial and her condemnation of anti-Catholic societies. In *Piam et constantem,* the Congregation for the Doctrine of the Faith stated:

> The reverent, unbroken practice of burying the bodies of the faithful departed is something the Church has always taken pains to encourage. It has surrounded the practice with rites suited to bring out more clearly the symbolic and religious significance of burial and has threatened with penalties those who might attack the sound practice. The Church has especially employed such sanctions in the face of hate-inspired assaults against Christian practices and traditions by those who, imbued with the animosity of their secret societies, sought to replace burial by cremation. . . .
>
> Cremation does not affect the soul nor prevent God's omnipotence from restoring the body; neither, then, does it in itself include an objective denial of the dogmas mentioned.

[4] Stanislaus Woywod, *A Practical Commentary on the Code of Canon Law* (New York: Joseph F. Wagner, 1932), 2:29.

The issue is not therefore an intrinsically evil act, opposed per se to the Christian religion. This has always been
the thinking of the Church: in certain situations where it
was or is clear that there is an upright motive for cremation, based on serious reasons, especially of public order,
the Church did not and does not object to it.

There has been a change for the better in attitudes and
in recent years more frequent and clearer situations imped-
ing the practice of burial have developed. Consequently,
the Holy See is receiving repeated requests for a relax-
ation of Church disciplines relative to cremation. The procedure is clearly being advocated today, not out of hatred
of the Church or Christian customs, but rather for reasons
of health, economics, or other reasons involving private or
public order.

It is the decision of the Church to accede to the requests
received, out of concern primarily for the spiritual well-
being of the faithful, but also out of its awareness of other
pressures.[5]

When *Piam et constantem* was written, less than 5 percent
of people chose cremation, but numbers have continued to
increase. Canon Law was updated in 1983, and canon 1184
removed cremation from the list of reasons to deny a Catholic funeral. As of today, Christian burial is denied only
to "notorious apostates, heretics, and schismatics . . . those
who chose cremation of their bodies for reasons contrary
to the Christian faith . . . [and] other manifest sinners."[6]

Over time, the cultural context continued to shift, and by
2018, the rate of cremation in the United States was 53.1
percent, ranging from a low of 26 percent (Mississippi) to

[5] Congregation for the Doctrine of Faith, Instruction on Cremation *Piam
et constantem* (May 8, 1963).

[6] Can. 1184 §1.

a high of 79.8 percent (Nevada).[7] The ultimate destiny of the cremated remains is equally divided among interment, scattering, or home preservation. In response to shifting cultural norms, in 2016 the Vatican once again reaffirmed its preference for burial:

> Following the most ancient Christian tradition, the Church insistently recommends that the bodies of the deceased be buried in cemeteries or other sacred places. . . .
>
> By burying the bodies of the faithful, the Church confirms her faith in the resurrection of the body, and intends to show the great dignity of the human body as an integral part of the human person whose body forms part of their identity.[8]

The Church, however, continues to permit cremation:

> When, for legitimate motives, cremation of the body has been chosen, the ashes of the faithful must be laid to rest in a sacred place. . . .
>
> From the earliest times, Christians have desired that the faithful departed become the objects of the Christian community's prayers and remembrance. Their tombs have become places of prayer, remembrance and reflection. The faithful departed remain part of the Church who believes "in the communion of all the faithful of Christ, those who are pilgrims on earth, the dead who are being purified, and the blessed in heaven, all together forming one Church". The reservation of the ashes of the departed in a sacred place ensures that they are not excluded from the prayers

[7] Cremation Association of North America, *CANA Annual Statistics Report*, 2018, https://cdn.ymaws.com/www.cremationassociation.org/resource/resmgr/members_statistics/CANA-2018StatsReport_3pg.pdf.

[8] Congregation for the Doctrine of Faith, Instruction Regarding the Burial of the Deceased and the Conservation of the Ashes in the Case of Cremation *Ad resurgendum cum Christo* (October 25, 2016), no. 3.

and remembrance of their family or the Christian community. It prevents the faithful departed from being forgotten, or their remains from being shown a lack of respect, which eventuality is possible, most especially once the immediately subsequent generation has too passed away. Also it prevents any unfitting or superstitious practices.[9]

In no uncertain terms, the Vatican condemned the spreading of ashes and choosing cremation as an expression of paganism:

> In order that every appearance of pantheism, naturalism or nihilism be avoided, it is not permitted to scatter the ashes of the faithful departed in the air, on land, at sea or in some other way, nor may they be preserved in mementos, pieces of jewellery or other objects. These courses of action cannot be legitimised by an appeal to the sanitary, social, or economic motives that may have occasioned the choice of cremation.
>
> When the deceased notoriously has requested cremation and the scattering of their ashes for reasons contrary to the Christian faith, a Christian funeral must be denied to that person according to the norms of the law.[10]

While Jed may have been well-intentioned in stuffing his friend's ashes into a shotgun barrel and blasting them over a pond of ducks, did this honor the dignity due to his friend's remains?

From this discussion there is no doubt that the Church has a preference for burial, but she recognizes that cremation is permissible for "legitimate motives". What constitutes a legitimate motive is not defined, but no doubt cost

[9] Congregation for the Doctrine of Faith, *Ad resurgendum cum Christo*, no. 5.

[10] Congregation for the Doctrine of Faith, *Ad resurgendum cum Christo*, nos. 7-8.

considerations can be a valid reason to choose cremation. In the United States, cremation can be roughly one-third the cost of burial, and for some families, the cost of burial is overly burdensome. While current Church law is accommodating toward this reality, it nevertheless does not *approve* of cremation but *permits* the practice: an important distinction.

Conclusion

To die well, one must live well. It seems fairly straightforward, yet life is full of spiritual and moral challenges that make living and dying well anything but easy. The essence of the good life is to cultivate the theological virtues of faith, hope, and charity, which are given to us at our Baptism. While our physical journey toward death begins at the moment of our birth, our spiritual preparation begins at Baptism. As St. Paul tells us, "Do you not know that all of us who have been baptized into Christ Jesus were baptized into his death? We were buried therefore with him by baptism into death, so that as Christ was raised from the dead by the glory of the Father, we too might walk in newness of life" (Rom 6:3–4). Our final destination is union with the Trinity in heaven. Death is the final and necessary step that brings us into true beatitude, so it makes sense for us to live our lives in preparation for this moment. Along the way, the Church stands ready to accompany us on this journey.

The measure of a "good death" in the eyes of the world is not the same for those who have faith in Christ. While a quiet, peaceful death is desirable, this is not the hallmark of a good death. To die well requires us to die to the world so that we may live to God, preparing ourselves to meet Christ. A good death is one that embraces the spiritual realities surrounding the process of dying; yet these realities have been largely ignored, and the decline of bodily function leading to death has become the primary focus of dying. Death has become "medicalized"; illness and death are the enemy, and modern technology are the weapons to defeat them.

In my experience as a neurosurgeon, patients and families are often overwhelmed by the complexity of medical decision making as death approaches. So much time is spent deciding things, that contemplation and prayer are pushed into the background. I hope that this book will encourage people to think about death and dying in advance, and will serve as a catalyst for conversation and prayer that helps us prepare to die well.

Index

brain death and, 55–56, 61–62

dignity of life and, 66

maternal death statistics, 67

maternal health, 67–70

maternal-fetal medicine, 65

neonatal death, 66

perinatal death, 65–75

perinatology, 68

preeclampsia, 67–68, 69

somatic support during pregnancy, 55–56

termination of, 72

unbaptized infants, 72–75, 196

uterine infection, 68, 69

premature babies

death of, 69

survival rates of, 68

pride, 108

psychological pain. *See also* suffering

drug use and, 127–28

Jesus Christ and, 167

presence of, 40

purgatory, 148n

purity/purification, 137, 148n, 151, 204

quarantine, 105, 106

Ratzinger, Joseph Cardinal, 56–57, 149, 158. *See also* Benedict XVI, Pope

Reconciliation. *See* Sacrament of Penance and Reconciliation

redemptive suffering, 166–71. *See also* suffering

Resurrection of Jesus Christ, 74, 155, 157, 158, 160, 187, 190, 195

resurrection of the dead, 56, 154, 155–57, 183, 184, 187, 190, 192, 194, 195, 199, 200n, 204

"right to die" ideology, 92

Rite of Committal, 195–96

Rite of Reception, 193

Rite of Viaticum, 91, 175, 176–77, 180–81, 182–85

Robert Bellarmine, Saint, 135, 138

the Rosary, 13, 141, 180, 182

Sacrament of Anointing of the Sick, 91, 147, 173–77, 183, 184

Sacrament of Penance and Reconciliation, 91, 137, 146, 173–77, 184. *See also* absolution

salvation

heaven and, 158

message of, 160

redemptive suffering and, 170

suffering and, 168

unbaptized infants and, 73–75

Salvifici doloris (apostolic letter) (John Paul II), 166–67, 168–69, 170

Saunders, Cicely, 39

Schiavo, Terri, 21

secularism, 86–87

self-determination, 49–50, 94

Sheol, 160